My Three Lives

My Three Lives

GORDON FERGUSON

A Story of One Man and Three Movements

My Three Lives
God's Relentless Pursuit
© 2016 by Gordon Ferguson

All rights are reserved. No part of this book may be duplicated, copied, translated, reproduced or stored mechanically, digitally or electronically without specific, written permission of the author and publisher.

Printed in the United States of America.

ISBN: 978-1-941988-44-2.

Unless otherwise indicated, all Scripture references are from THE HOLY BIBLE, NEW INTERNATIONAL VERSION®, NIV® Copyright © 1973, 1978, 1984, 2011 by Biblica, Inc.® Used by permission. All rights reserved worldwide.

Cover and interior book design: Toney Mulhollan. The book interior is set in Minion Pro and Arial Narrow.

Thank you to Amy Morgan and Gina Poirer for their editorial help.

Illumination Publishers cares deeply for the environment and uses recycled papers whenever possible.

Illumination Publishers titles may be purchased in bulk for classroom instruction, business, fund-raising, or sales promotional use. For information please e-mail paul.ipibooks@me.com.

About the author: Gordon Ferguson is a graduate of Northwestern State University and the Harding School of Theology. With more than forty-five years of experience, he has served as an evangelist, elder and teacher. He emphasizes leadership training and teaching. Gordon has also written fourteen books and many audio and video teaching series. Gordon and his wife, Theresa, reside in McKinney, Texas. For more articles, additional information, and speaking schedules, go to Gordon's website at www.GordonFerguson.org.

CONTENTS

ACKNOWLEDGEMENTS 7

FOREWORD 8

INTRODUCTION: God's Relentless Pursuit 10

PART ONE:
AN ODD CHURCH OF CHRIST AND MY RIOTOUS LIVING

Chapter 1: Spiritual Weirdness and My Family Background 14
Chapter 2: Doctrinal Weirdness and My Early Years 22
Chapter 3: A Character for a Mother, Thankfully 27
Chapter 4: Thank God for the Bright Spots! 34

PART TWO:
THE MAINLINE CHURCH OF CHRIST AND MY LEGALISM

Chapter 5: My Baptist Wife and Religious Strife 40
Chapter 6: Amazing Breakthroughs 46
Chapter 7: Ministry Training as Student and Teacher 53
Chapter 8: Wild Adventures—Almost Too Young and Too Soon 63
Chapter 9: A Growing Disenchantment 69

PART THREE:
THE DISCIPLING MOVEMENT AND MY WILDEST ADVENTURE YET

Chapter 10: A Phone Call from an Angel 84
Chapter 11: A Blizzard and the State of Shock 91
Chapter 12: The Good, the Bad and the Ugly 96
Chapter 13: From the Frying Pan into the Fire 109
Chapter 14: A Growing Disenchantment, Revisited 119
Chapter 15: God Help Us with Solutions! 135

Dedication

In memory of the five people who were the greatest influence in my early years, on me as a person and later as a spiritual person, all used by God to help mold me into who I became in my later years.

My father, *Byrle Ferguson,* who instilled in me a determination to always tell the truth and the fighter's spirit to follow through no matter the consequences.

My mother, *Violet Ferguson*, who instilled in me an unshakable trust in the Bible as the word of God and helped develop me into somewhat of a character.

My first spiritual mentor, *Richard Hostetler*, who instilled in me the love of Jesus and a burning desire to preach.

My second spiritual mentor, *Eldred Stevens*, who through his faith in me, instilled in me a desire to be a teacher and trainer of ministers and first gave me the opportunity to do it in an academic setting.

My third spiritual mentor, *J.T. Bristow*, who through his training and example, instilled in me the gift of motivational preaching.

To these five, and all since whose influence has built upon their foundation, I will be eternally grateful.

Acknowledgements

Although this list could be quite long, I will limit it to those whose work behind the scenes made this book a reality. Writing three books in the space of four months has been a daunting task for an old guy like me. Getting them to publication was just as challenging for Toney Mulhollan and Amy Morgan, and perhaps more so. Toney has given me much input and direction, besides having to design covers and set type for these books. I told him that he reminded me of a movie title, *Ex Machina*, for he is like a machine in doing all that he does. Amy has been of inestimable editing help through many years, especially in helping me get my most important leadership book, *Dynamic Leadership*, translated into Spanish. She has also been the main copyeditor for my current three books. She has been a delight to work with. Gina Poirier has done the final read on these books and manages to catch the things that the rest of us miss. She has been a valuable and appreciated part of the team. All my love and appreciation to you three. Special thanks to my wife, Theresa, for her gracious support and tolerance of my rather intense writer's stress during the past four months!

Foreword

My first meeting with Gordon Ferguson was in January 1983 after I had ridden an Amtrak train across the country to speak at a conference directed by the Poway Church of Christ in the San Diego area. I had read a few articles by Gordon and had seen his name in some publications associated with the Churches of Christ. He was from Tacoma, Washington, and was also there to speak for the conference. As God would have it, the two of us were assigned to share a hotel room together, quite unaware that this would be the beginning of a friendship that has now lasted for thirty-three years.

The meeting that brought us together was part of a growing spiritual reform effort that was often called the Crossroads or Discipling Movement. Neither of us had come from the church in Gainesville, Florida, that had given birth to this fresh emphasis on regaining the essentials of biblical discipleship. However, at different points we had both been influenced by this movement and had found in it many kindred spirits.

Four years later, and after several moves by both of us, God's providence would lead to our families living in the Boston suburb of Bedford, Massachusetts, and less than four years after that the two of us would begin to work together as writer and editor with Discipleship Publications International (DPI), the new publishing arm of the Boston Church of Christ.

As I have written in my own memoir, my friendship with Gordon has been and continues to be a great source of faith, encouragement and strength in my life. He is the real deal, and I am blessed that God brought me into his sphere of influence. As you will see in this book, after a raucous beginning in which there was a crazy (he will say "weird") mixture of leniency and legalism, he made a decision to surrender to Jesus, and having put hand to plow, has never looked back. He has gone on to be one of clearest voices in our day for the compassion and grace of God that leads to all-out and complete commitment.

A plainspoken fellow who sees no need for fancy words, Gordon does not leave you guessing at what he thinks. As I read the manuscript, I could not help but think how my father would have loved this book. I can just hear him saying to me, "Son, your friend Gordon knows how to put the hay down where the goats can get it." The straight talk we get from Gordon is sometimes linked with a wacky sense of humor and holds lots of practical insights about living out the Kingdom of God—life as God intended it.

No doubt many of you have read other books by Gordon and felt their impact. A great many of you have heard him speak and remember that it was with passion and power. But then there is something special about getting to know that person you have read or heard and coming away with a better grasp of how the hand of God wove the different strands of their life together to make them the person they are.

As you read, you will not only get to know Gordon better, you will gain insight into some of our roots, into the spiritual movement you may be part of, and into yourself and your own walk with God. I can commend this work to you as one I think you will enjoy. You will come away with a greater appreciation for the Bible. Your faith will grow. You will hear praise for God's grace, but before you are done, you will know a strong challenge has come to your life. With Gordon, it could not be any other way.

—Tom A. Jones
Nashville, Tennessee

Introduction

God's Relentless Pursuit

Gordon Ferguson

"What made you decide to write this book?" I've been asked that question or similar ones many times. It's a good question and one I always enjoy having to think about at least a little before answering. The interesting thing is that each book demands somewhat of a different answer. I started off writing books by first writing study booklets, in extended outline format using complete sentences. Several of these I have expanded into regular, full-length books; and another half dozen I never did, although some of them were almost long enough to be books in total word count. If I considered them as books, along with my others, the total number of books I have authored would be nearly twenty. I wrote each one for a different reason, although some of them for related reasons. As is my custom (I think in imitating Jesus in his storytelling), I will answer the question about my reason for writing this book by telling the backstory.

Sometime in early April 2007, I received an email from my very special friend, Tom Jones, with a manuscript of a book attached and a request to read it and give him my opinion. I procrastinated in fulfilling his request, for several reasons. One, I was working on a very intense project of my own at the time. Two, I perceived that his book proposal involved writing a history of the International Church of Christ, which I didn't feel good about. Writing histories, especially of young movements, is often said to be something that should be saved for later when the perspectives have stood the test of more passage of time. But my reticence was more involved than that—I was fearful that his book might reignite critical attitudes toward leaders, which I thought we had experienced too much of already. However, in spite of my hesitation, I felt obligated to read his manuscript, since he had read many of mine as the former editor of Discipleship Publications International (DPI).

Once I began, I was mesmerized as I read the manuscript of what was to become a book entitled *In Search of a City*.[1] My concerns going in were soon totally dispatched. He was not as critical of ICOC history as I may well be in this present book! Tom is always very evenhanded when offering criticisms, which are always constructive. Further, in reading his work, it was obvious that his book was not claiming to be a history of the movement, but a history of Tom Jones' experience in the movement—two very different things. I told him that my bottom line opinion of his book was this: "You did a masterful job of staying very honest and evenhanded in a way that very few could do, and yours truly is not among that number. I would not trust myself to do it, but you did it extremely well." As some of my teacher/author friends and I discussed Tom's book after publication, it was suggested by one of them that I write something similar about my own history. Others encouraged me as well. I thought of a title pretty quickly, but for whatever reasons, am just now getting around to the task of writing the book. Being seventy-three years old helps you realize that if you are going to share your history you had better do it sooner than later, before you become history yourself! Hence, the book comes now.

Everyone has a different personal history in many aspects, and certainly this is true in the spiritual realm. When we share our spiritual history, we do share historical facts about whatever religious group or movement we have been a part of, and some of these facts would otherwise remain unknown. While we are writing about our own experiences, we provide insights into that church history which should be preserved and otherwise would not be. Tom's book certainly did that, based on the path he followed that eventually led him into the ICOC. I followed a very different path, although we ended up in the same movement of churches and share many similarities in beliefs and overall life experiences. But for each of us, and for every other church leader or member, our stories are unique to us. That fact is remarkable in and of itself. No two humans are just alike—period.

I chose the title of this book for a very definite reason: I have lived in three very different religious settings, each with its own cast of characters and belief systems that varied from one another in very unique ways. I was also probably influenced by the title of an old TV show of yesteryear, *My Three Sons*. I will guarantee you several things as you read the book. One, you will learn a lot more about me than you already knew, in spite of my having been very open and vulnerable in my oral and written teaching for decades. Two, you will learn a lot more about the spiritual movements of which I have been a part than you already knew, including some very interesting details indeed. Three, you will develop a deeper appreciation for God and a more heartfelt awe of him as you see how he has worked in my life.

The book is about me and my experiences in one sense, but in the greater sense, it is a book about a God who relentlessly pursues us, no matter what that pursuit involves. Thus, the subtitle of the book is really the point that I most want you to walk away with after you finish reading. I had, and you have, a God of relentless pursuit. He wants a personal relationship with us and did not hesitate to pay the highest price imaginable in order to get us: an old rugged cross on Golgotha's hill. Even when we may have been far from being interested in pursuing him, he has always been pursuing us whether or not we had any clue about it at all. When we finally start pursuing him, won over by his love, I picture his heart warming, his face smiling and his mind thinking, "It was worth it." I pray that my book makes you and God smile. If that happens, my mind will similarly think, "My writing efforts were worth it," a pitifully weak comparison to his efforts on our behalf, but nonetheless encouraging to me. Enjoy the read!

---

1. Thomas A. Jones, *In Search of a City: An Autobiographical Perspective on a Remarkable but Controversial Movement* (Spring Hill, TN: DPI Books, 2007).

PART ONE:
AN ODD CHURCH OF CHRIST AND MY RIOTOUS LIVING

Chapter One

Spiritual Weirdness and My Family Background

I was born to a strange set of parents, and always wondered how they got together in the first place. My father's immediate family, consisting of two parents and four brothers, was one composed of unvarnished pagans. They were as worldly as worldly could be, and never went inside a church building except for weddings and funerals. By the admission of one of my dad's younger brothers, they exited as quickly as possible when these events were over because, as the old Southern saying goes, they were as nervous as a long-tailed cat in a room full of rocking chairs. After they were married, my oldest uncle and my dad did start to attend church some through the influence of their wives, but I didn't see much difference between them and my younger uncles. My mother's immediate family was one made up of very religious folks when I entered the world on October 27, 1942. Mother had a widowed mother, one sister and two brothers. They were religious, but weird religious. Given that strange combination from which to choose, I chose the pagan side of the family with which to identify. My uncles were my heroes and my role models. I imitated the way they talked, the way they walked and the way they viewed the world. Of course, that view determined their actions—and mine.

William Guy Ashley

My mother's father (William Guy Ashley) had been a preacher but died at age thirty-three, leaving behind a young wife with four small children. My mother was the next to youngest among her siblings and only about three years old when her father died. She really had no memories of him.

My grandmother decided to remain single "to honor her departed husband's memory," a decision with disastrous consequences, to say nothing of flatly disobeying what the Bible says in 1 Timothy 5:14: *"So I counsel younger widows to marry, to have children, to manage their homes and to give the enemy no opportunity for slander."* She made that decision at a very young age and never wavered from it, which was also a decision to raise four children through the Great Depression in the United States with virtually no money and no clear way to earn a living. As I said, it was a disastrous decision that left three of the four children, including my mother, with significant emotional damage.

How I Ended Up in Louisiana

As I recall the story, my mother's family was living in East Texas and came over to Shreveport, Louisiana for my grandfather to preach a "gospel meeting." Those events had been popular for decades, and in their earliest years, dating back to the frontier days, they were very effective in baptizing people. It was how most churches known as Churches of Christ conducted their evangelistic outreach. During those frontier days in the late 1700s and beyond, a visiting preacher came to town and preached for a set period of time each night and on Sundays. In the early days, the meetings could last for several weeks. By the time I entered the world, they were two weeks long, and eventually they came to last a week or only a weekend. At any rate, the sermons were designed to convert visitors, and the members were to bring their friends and neighbors for this purpose. As I said, in the early days, these meetings were very effective. Most of the population lived in rural settings and there wasn't much else to do for entertainment anyway, so going to church was an enticing opportunity. Sometimes the meetings took place in available buildings like schools, since church buildings were small, or they were held under tents or brush arbors. Brush arbors were easy to construct, using freshly felled trees, with the tree trunks making up the poles, smaller tree trunks or limbs forming the roof rafters, and small limbs with leaves intact spread across the rafters to complete the structure. From what I understand, they blocked both sun and rain fairly effectively, depending on the skill of the builders. The seats were made from larger split logs with legs made of smaller logs. I actually saw one of these when I was a young adult, although it was only for exhibition purposes, having been long extinct as functioning meeting places for "brush-arbor meetings."

I don't know where that Church of Christ met in Shreveport where my grandfather came to preach back in the early 1920s, but I do know that he contracted typhoid fever and died in a short time. The leaders of the little church felt terrible about what had happened and invited my grandmother to move her young family to Shreveport, with a promise to try and help take care of them. Whatever financial care they offered was scant, based on the stories my mother told of growing up having to keep the soles of her shoes intact with the help of chewing gum. I think it wasn't so much the children being without money and a father that marked them so much emotionally; it was my grandmother's attitude and disposition. She was an unhappy woman with a bitter spirit residing just beneath the surface. My opinion is that she had a mindset that didn't allow her to question God and work through her grief by so doing, so she just kept it all inside and did what she believed to be the spiritual thing. She showed her two sons much more love than she did her two daughters, but my oldest uncle was the only one that could be honestly called normal.

In spite of it all, my grandmother was very committed to her religion, which was a strange religion indeed. More about that in the next chapter. Her church may have been called a Church of Christ, but it bore little resemblance to what I call the mainline Church of Christ. The root system of the Churches of Christ traced back to what is known as the Restoration Movement. The more familiar Reformation Movement, with figures like Martin Luther and John Calvin as key players, began as an attempt to reform the Catholic Church. Churches in this movement became known in time as Protestant churches because they were protesting Catholic Church practices. However, by 1700, there were about 150 different "flavors" of churches within Protestantism. The early Restoration pronounced failure upon the Reformation Movement because of these doctrinal differences and resultant divisions. Hence came the idea, a rather noble one actually, to just start over, follow the Bible and restore the original church that you read about in the New Testament.

Legalism Gone to Seed

The goal of following the Bible was certainly the right call, but just what should that mean? How closely should the Bible be followed, taking into consideration the differences in doctrines intended to be eternal and customs and practices intended only to be temporary for the first-century culture? That has been a debate ever since the inception of the Restoration Movement. For example, in 1 Corinthians 11, women were forbidden to worship in assemblies without their heads being covered. In the church of my youth, this was taken literally and all of the women wore hats in church services, most with veils attached to cover their faces. In many congregations, "pattern theology" won the day when it came to biblical interpretation. The pattern meant that everything, or almost everything, in the New Testament was to be taken literally and followed literally. Whatever the early church did, we had to do. From this mindset came the popular slogan of the Restoration Movement, "Where the Bible speaks we speak, and where the Bible is silent, we are silent." That may sound both reasonable and noble, but it led to some amazing outcomes and divisions galore.

I once read a pamphlet identifying 100 types of variations within the Churches of Christ. Some of the practices, defended staunchly as "sound doctrine," are both shocking and sometimes humorous. Certain churches actually build their buildings on stilts because Jesus and the early church met in an "upstairs room" (Luke 22:12; Acts 1:13; Acts 20:8). No, I am not kidding. Certain churches wouldn't allow kitchens to be built in their buildings, since Paul said in 1 Corinthians 11:22: *"Don't you have homes to eat and drink in? Or do you despise the church of God by humiliating those who have nothing? What shall I say to you? Shall I praise you? Certainly not in this matter!"* He also said in the same chapter: *"Anyone who is hungry should eat something at home, so that when you meet together it may not result in judgment"* (1 Corinthians 11:34a).

Of course, when you study the context, they were meeting in

houses and were indeed eating meals together. The issue was that the rich folks came early and gobbled up all of the food, whereas the poor (most of whom were slaves and couldn't come until after work) missed out on the meal. The chapter is so clear on this point that you marvel that anyone could have ever hatched the idea that eating in church buildings was wrong, but that is where pattern theology and terrible exegesis (interpretation of a biblical text) brings you. One old preacher that I met when I was young was known for both his quick wit and sharp tongue. His crude comment about this doctrine was that those folks wouldn't build kitchens in their buildings so as to ensure that food couldn't be taken in, but they built bathrooms so that you could let it out! The list of such well-intentioned doctrines and practices is long, being tragic and humorous to us moderns at the same time. But I was born in the middle of this religions climate, partially explaining my attraction to the world because of the weirdness of the churches—many of them at least, certainly including the one my mother dragged me to.

A Deeper Source of Legalism

Pattern theology did its own damage in producing widespread divisions within Churches of Christ, but a deeper problem was biblical ignorance and terrible theology. Most of the preachers up until more modern times were self-educated. Some were highly intelligent and avid readers of the Bible and of other spiritual books, and were far more on track in their approach to interpretation. However, those were not the preachers of my childhood. Those I knew, however noble their purposes may have been, were poor expositors of the Bible. In their attempts to take the Bible literally (a valid idea combined with sensible contextual exposition), they took scriptures out of their contexts. Some of their poor exegesis was reasonably harmless and some of it was extremely harmful, resulting in distorted views of God and religion in general.

For example, James made this comment in a context condemning the act of showing favoritism toward rich visitors to services: *"For whoever keeps the whole law and yet stumbles at just one point is guilty of breaking all of it"* (James 2:10). If you read the context, it is apparent that he is saying that you cannot justify showing favoritism by using the passage about loving your neighbor as yourself while breaking the scripture about showing favoritism. If you violate one scripture, you have gone over the line and broken the law, regardless of which type of violation broke the law. The interpretation I was taught as a young boy was that when you sin in any way, you are guilty of having broken the whole law—meaning that you are then guilty of every sin mentioned in the Bible. Not only is that a perfectly erroneous interpretation of the verse, it produces a type of legalism that all but destroys the possibility of loving church or loving God. It heaps guilt on top of guilt to the point of making one absolutely paranoid about doing anything wrong. It makes the last part of Romans 7 look like a stroll in the park. Yet, that is what I was raised to believe. You can see why Romans became my favorite book in the Bible, for it was my key to spiritual freedom and a positive view of God.

World, Here I Come!

Now you understand my religious family and why I was strongly drawn to my father's pagan family. Religion for me was "hellfire and brimstone" to the nth degree. I hated it, and I had such a fear of God and of Judgment Day that I tried to put it all out of my mind as much as possible. Riotous living helped. I won't go into all of the types of sin my pagan uncles introduced me to, but not much was left out, and it started at a young age. For example, during holiday season, popping firecrackers was a big deal to youngsters back then. My grandparents had a storm cellar in their backyard that stuck out of the ground about four feet. It was my favorite place from which to light and throw firecrackers. (I'm surprised I managed to keep all of my fingers intact, looking back at it.) One of my dad's younger brothers provided me with cigars to smoke and light my firecrackers with. I was all of seven years old. My grandmother was watching me from the kitchen window and thought nothing of it. I was the first grandchild, and my youngest uncle was only ten years older than I. In effect, I was the fifth Ferguson boy and could do no wrong in their eyes (God's eyes being quite another matter!).

My youngest uncle introduced me to pornography at a very early age. He had Playboy-type magazines around the house in plain view, and again, Grandma had no objection. He started smoking very young, likely before his teenage years, but all of that was a part of the Ferguson culture, and I was a Ferguson. I followed in their steps in every way I could and, unfortunately, succeeded in doing so. I was completely turned off to religion and completely turned on to sin. I remember singing a different version of an old church hymn with my buddies (and you know which kind of friends I chose). The actual wording of the song had a stanza in it that said, "We were sinking deep in sin, far from the peaceful shore." We sang, "We are sinking deep in sin—whee!" When I say I had a lot to overcome to get within shouting distance of spirituality, I am not exaggerating in the least.

The Embarrassment Factor

When I say that all things religious were highly embarrassing to me, I expect you are starting to get the point. You will gain a far better understanding in the next chapter. I encountered my first church division at age five and actually remember it pretty well. We were in a small church already, with perhaps 150 people attending on a given Sunday. But we split over what seemed to be a nonsensical matter: one of our friends became a bit too broad-minded; when he baptized people, he just sent them to the Church of Christ nearest their home, even if it was a different "flavor" than ours. That led to him being disfellowshipped, and when one of our closer friends spoke up against it, he too was disfellowshipped on the spot. Those of you with little or no personal experience with the divisive elements of Church of Christ history, be thankful. Our religious side of the family formed a new congregation of about twenty people with the second fellow who had been put out of the church. He was a postman by trade and our new preacher. We met in his home for some months, then in a rented, rundown Boy Scout hut, and ultimately we built a little, square frame church building in my neighborhood.

Most of the people in my hometown of Shreveport went to church on Sunday mornings. It was a Bible Belt city called "The City of Churches," and that it was. Therefore, almost everyone I knew went to church on Sundays. We may have been drunk and partying the night before (I and my set of friends certainly were), but we were dressed in our Sunday best the next morning, sitting on hard pews (designed to keep you awake) while being bored to death. I brought the art of daydreaming to near perfection as a result of those Sunday meetings, an art that has served me well even as an adult in certain situations. I can tune out crying babies, barking dogs, people giving me unwanted lectures, etc. with the best of 'em. The worst part was that most of my friends attended big Baptist or Methodist Churches, and I attended a weird little church that met in a cracker-box-type of little building. I was embarrassed by even going to church. After services, I'd wait until my parents were outside getting into the car before I went out and hastily got in the car with them. After all, my church was in my neighborhood and I didn't want any of my friends to see me.

My weird religion carried over into other parts of my life as well, often in embarrassing ways. I joined the Boy Scouts when I was in the sixth grade—for three weeks. The Scoutmaster planned a camping trip for a Friday and Saturday night, with us returning late Sunday afternoon. We were going to attend a Methodist church that Sunday morning near the campground. However, my mother wouldn't let me go. After all, did not Hebrews 10:25 say: "...not giving up meeting together, as some are in the habit of doing, but encouraging one another—and all the more as you see the day approaching"? That meant to my mother and those in my church that you couldn't ever miss a Sunday unless you were really sick. To attend another type of church was unthinkable, for they were not doctrinally sound (even for a twelve-year-old). Weird, huh? I met one guy when we were adults who was raised in a church slightly right of mine on the doctrinal scale of weirdness, who said that his family saw only two churches in the whole country as true churches. Hence, they had to vacation every year at the other town in order to avoid forsaking the assembly and to avoid attending an unsound church. Being from California, his family had to vacation in Illinois. I suppose the Illinois church members were happy that their only sister church was in California! So, if you think I'm weird (and I am, actually), at least I came by it honestly!

Chapter Two

Doctrinal Weirdness and My Early Years

By this point, you've already read enough to believe me when I say I was raised in a weird church. However, until you read this chapter, you have no idea just how weird it was. So here we go. As you know by now, the earlier Churches of Christ came in many variations, "flavors" if you will. Mine was called a one-cup, no-Sunday school Church of Christ. "Well Gordon, what in the world was that?" Very good question; very sad answer.

One-Cuppers

We used one cup for communion, and one bread tray as well. Does the Bible not describe Jesus' institution of the Lord's Supper as him taking "the" cup? It doesn't say anywhere that he took multiple cups. If we are one body, one family, should we not be united and show our unity in communion, of all things? So goes the argument in its most basic form. "That's crazy," you are thinking, right? Of course, it is, but let me say this: I would not debate a one-cupper debater today without adequate time to prepare. I have attended a number of such debates on subjects like this one, and you would be shocked at the amount of arguments they call into play and the seeming logic of said arguments. Good debaters can make almost any position in religion or politics sound both true and reasonable. Be careful in dealing with religious people who know their doctrines well, even if they are false. A skilled person might end up tying you in knots. I've been there myself on the wrong end of that rope. But yes, it's a crazy doctrine, and this movement of churches has all but died out. Needless to say, very few of the second generation remained in that group, if in any church at all. Weirdness repels.

So, one-cuppers use one cup for communion. But it's not as

simple as that. What goes in that one cup—unfermented grape juice or wine? There were two movements at one time, each holding to a different answer for that question. Some were one-cuppers using wine and some were one-cuppers using grape juice. My little group started off as grape-juice users. However, we knew of a couple who lived near where we met and yet drove to another town where there was a wine-using one-cup church. So, our preaching postman (one of the few sincere guys in that little group) came up with the idea that we should change over to wine so that we could increase our number. Evangelistic outreach was not a part of our church, as far as I ever knew, but enticing a family of members was exciting to some of our group and anathema to others. We debated this for at least six months. Since half the members were my relatives, it was an interesting sight to behold. Most discussions shed far more heat than light on the subject.

My mother was leaning toward the wine position when we had an old preacher friend from Texas come for a visit. He always stayed with us, I think because he rather enjoyed my mother's outstanding culinary skills. At any

My parents: Byrle and Violet Ferguson

rate, I remember a discussion in our living room that well confirms my description of biblical ignorance in that fellowship. Mother said, "Well, Doug, the Bible does use the word 'wine' a lot." Of course, in the King James Version the word "wine" just meant the juice of the grape, whether fermented or unfermented. But Mother didn't know that fact. Doug's reply was the corker. He said, with a raised voice full of agitation, "Yes it does, and it also uses the word 'hellfire' a lot, but it doesn't say to put it on the Lord's Table!" In the end, we opted to switch over to using wine, and on the first Sunday we put it into practice, one family of four left us and one family of four joined us. So much for growth by trying to entice new members through changing our doctrine.

There was humor involved in it all, looking back. I remember one preacher in the mainline church telling about his similar background to mine, being also raised in a one-cup church. He was a funny guy to start with, and in his sermon he described his background and then what happened when his uncle developed tuberculous. He said that they went from being one-cuppers to two-cuppers overnight! I recall attending our old church in Dallas, where we had lived for three years when I was a very young child. I was a teenager at the service described and it was Easter Sunday. Everyone was dressed to the hilt, especially the women (as is usually the case!), and the church building was packed. In the 1950s in Dallas, segregation was firmly entrenched and very rarely discussed publicly. It was the accepted order of the day. That morning just as the services were starting, a black woman, dressed really well, entered the building. That in itself created some mumbling and craned necks looking back. All of the pews were full, so one of the men put a folding chair in the back, right in the middle aisle. That meant that half of the church drank out of that one cup before she did and the other half drank out of it after she did. Knowing well the bigotry of the day, I couldn't help but laugh to myself as I imagined what some were thinking as they followed her in drinking from the cup. Since I actually do have some African blood in me (twelve percent, according to a DNA test), I always looked at black people differently than many did then and hated the prejudices. That woman had guts to even come to that service. I hope God blessed her!

No Sunday School

If you took communion from one cup, that didn't mean you were one of the faithful few on your way to heaven. You also had to be in a church that didn't separate the children out of the services. After all, doesn't 1 Corinthians 14:23 speak of the "whole church" coming together? Where do you see any example in the New Testament of children's classes? That was a modern invention, not a Bible example, after all! The Sunday School Movement began in Britain in the 1780s, started by the English Anglican evangelical Robert Raikes (1725–1811), and it soon spread to the United States. I knew that bit of important history as a young child. All kinds of arguments are still being made (for different reasons) about whether the children should be in the services with their parents or not, and at some age, they of course should. But I'm all for Sunday school, or children's ministry as we typically call it in our movement of churches. Whatever the argument, don't misuse the Bible to make your points. The Bible leaves out more details than it contains, even in spiritual areas. The good Lord evidently expected us to use our common sense to figure out how to best meet the spiritual needs of his family, regardless of age. Important doctrines are established and essential; practical implementations are left up to us in large part.

Church buildings didn't exist in the early centuries of the church. They were a persecuted people and met in private places, much like illegal churches meet in some countries today. However, with time, after the intense persecution ended, church buildings started being built and eventually became cathedrals costing shameful amounts of money. As I drive through Dallas today, I don't see cathedrals per se, but without question, I see many church buildings that cost shameful amounts of money to build. We will develop that story later in the book. Along with building those early church buildings, certain doctrines started developing—false ones. The word "church" itself came to mean the building, as in "Where is your church located?" Then the buildings became holy places, much like the temple in Old Testament times. In the early Restoration Movement, especially among the stranger type groups, we developed the sanctuary idea (meaning "set apart" for holy purposes). This led to the resistance to eating in the building among some groups. It also led to not using the building for any kind of meeting except for the "whole church" assemblies. Therefore, some churches built separate buildings for the women to meet in for their ladies' Bible classes, usually held on Wednesday mornings. After all, we wouldn't want our sisters to defile the sanctuary, would we?

Praise God for Human Flexibility

For those of you reading this who actually find it familiar, I feel sorry for you. For those of you raised in other groups that were day-and-night different, yet taught false doctrines of other types, I feel sorry for you too. Don't laugh at my background religious experiences and I won't laugh at yours—deal? The truth is that Satan is a liar and the father of lies and loves false doctrines. He has invented hundreds of them, probably thousands. Some seem much more reasonable than others, yet they don't match up with biblical teaching and are therefore false. Those that seem ludicrous, like the ones in my background, still did untold damage. Paul uses the words "sound doctrine" several times. Sound means "healthy" or "that which produces health" and doctrine simply means "teaching." Thus, sound doctrine is teaching that makes us healthy spiritually. False doctrines do the very opposite, and millions become so angry and disillusioned by what they have experienced that they give up on God and church altogether. That is so, so sad.

But praise God for human flexibility, tolerance and adaptability. Many of you reading this book had to escape from some form of false teaching. Some of you raised in this present movement, the one of which I am a part also, still have misconceptions about God and things spiritual. Spirituality is a matter of basically loving God and imitating Jesus. It's not complicated, but it's not easy either. The wonderful blessing for which we can all give thanks is that the Bible is the most practical handbook for life that ever will be written. It works; it changes us; it reprograms our thinking; it is God speaking to us—his love letter to us. And whatever he asks for in our lives, he will enable us to do it and be it. It will take time and effort and failures and repentance, but it will happen. Some changes belong to repentance and can come fast. New converts demonstrate that fact well. Other changes belong to spiritual growth and may take a lot of time, but unless we just give up and quit, we will keep changing for a lifetime. Weirdness may never be completely overcome, but it can be kept in reasonable check, and working on doing that makes life interesting. God was somewhere in my crazy religious background, as he was in yours (whatever it was) and he is with us now. You can laugh or cry about your background; I choose to laugh (at least in this chapter)! No matter what, God's pursuit of us is relentless, based on his timetable.

Chapter Three

A Character for a Mother, Thankfully

My mother, now deceased, had the emotional baggage I mentioned in Chapter 1, but was she a character! I like the advertising byline for one TV show, "Characters Welcome." The slogan was adopted in 2005 by USA Network and has been used ever since. At that time the network was best known for its original program, *Monk*, which was about an obsessive-compulsive detective, and the mix of comedic characters in detective shows became USA's trademark. They have followed it with show after show with similar formulas and to positive reviews from most critics. I think they should pay me some kind of finder's fee since my mother lived by that motto. She was a character, she loved characters and she obviously turned me into one. In spite her legalistic views of Christianity, her craziness helped to provide some kind of balancing point for me as I grew up. I was almost totally turned off by her religious views, but other than that, life with her was often fun.

There's Not Always Fun in Dysfunction

Our immediate family was dysfunctional, but it was better than most of the families in our extended list of relatives. I mentioned that my one grandfather was a preacher and died very young, with disastrous consequences for those left behind. I've often wondered why he had to die so young, and of course I'll never know the answer to that question this side of eternity. But for us humans, it's difficult (nearly impossible) to avoid speculating. One of my speculations involves my grandfather's family. All of them started out in those little one-cup, no-Sunday-school churches. Excepting my great-grandparents, they all left the church at some point, all becoming characters and some becoming criminals. One of my great-uncles (brother of my dead preacher grandfather) killed his wife, claiming that he did it accidentally while cleaning his gun for a hunting trip. I fished with him a few times, but I don't remember him ever talking about hunting. He and his wife were both alcoholics and had a terrible marriage. Most in the family believed that he murdered her and then was a good enough actor in court to be found innocent. He later stole his brother's wife while living with them, and all three of them lived under the same roof afterward for many years, on apparently good terms. That was further along on the weird scale than the suspected murder, at least to me.

The third brother was a con artist who bilked rich widows out of their money in Los Angeles. He was either driving a Cadillac about half a block long or in jail, going back and forth between the two lifestyles. All of the brothers were very intelligent, and I suspect that my intellectual capabilities and writing abilities came from their side of the family. Back to my speculation about my grandfather's early death: perhaps he died young so as not to get caught up in the ungodly directions of his brothers, thus making it possible for my grandmother and mother to stick with their brand of spirituality. Whatever else may be said, those two women had no questions about the Bible being the word of God, and that part was passed on to me—whether I wanted it at the time or not. Simply put, I couldn't escape that conclusion, even with great effort at times.

The Bible Is True

One of my favorite hymns is "Ancient Words."[2] I like Michael W. Smith's version of it because of the bagpipes. I am part Scot, with both my first and last name having an official Scottish plaid connected to them. Look up the song on the Internet; the words are worth carefully listening to or reading. They express what I feel and believe about the Bible: "Ancient words ever true, changing me and changing you." The Bible has changed my life and my eternity. To me, those ancient words are indeed ever true, changing me and changing you (if we let them). Even in my rebellious years, I never doubted their veracity; nor do I now. I've read liberal books of all sorts that have shaken or destroyed the faith of many, but I still say with Paul, *"Let God be true, and every human being a liar"* (Romans 3:4). The Bible is true. I would bet my life on it. I *have* bet my life—and eternity—on it. And I have my grandmother and mother to thank for that.

Of course, I also have some of their views (mis)taken from the Bible to thank them for as well, although "thank" is not the most accurate word to use in this regard. The legalism of our religion gave my mother a distorted view of God and his teaching. She always spoke in very fear-inducing terms of eternity and meeting God. Hell became far more real to me than heaven as a result. I remember her sharing a sin-list passage with me once, really emphasizing the sin of immorality. She explained it in a way that left it in my mind as the unforgiveable sin. Once you'd done it, that was it—you were headed to hell. I hadn't committed that sin yet (one of my few omissions in the whole list), but my friend Ronnie had. I remember that we were in the eighth grade when he lost his virginity. I can vividly recall my thinking at that moment when listening to my mother's lecture. It went something like this: "Ronnie is done for, and no matter what else happens in the rest of his life, he is bound for hell." It was that lack of grace that filled me with fear of death and the judgment to come. I don't think we sang that old song in our church that has the line, "There's an all-seeing Eye watching you,"[3] but we surely believed it and feared it mightily.

Gordon Ferguson-age 4. Destined for trouble at an early age.

Mother Had Help (Of the Wrong Kind)

It wasn't just Mother who gave me a distorted view of biblical teaching. She had one other unfortunate ally in this—the visiting preacher who spoke of not having wine or hellfire on the Lord's Table. His name was Doug, and he was basically a nice guy. I daydreamed during our regular preacher's lessons. I honestly don't have one memory from any of his many sermons wasted on me. Doug, however, was hard to ignore. He was a preacher about the end times, and his sermons about Gog, Magog, the Great Tribulation and Armageddon scared me half to death. As stated earlier, he loved my mother's cooking. His favorite meal was fried catfish, hush puppies and French fries, washed down by copious amounts of lemonade. Sweet ice tea was the beverage of choice in our house (I had a different choice outside our house, of course), but Doug had to have his lemonade.

Just after John F. Kennedy was elected president, Doug came for a visit and had a chat with Mother before dinner. Shortly after their chat, Mother informed me of the content of their conversation. I remember exactly where I was standing in the kitchen as she shared the horrifying details with me.

Gordon Ferguson-age 10. Boots were still in style for manly footwear.

The battle of Armageddon was at hand, to be fought between the United States and Russia, since Russia and the Catholic Church were Gog and Magog (and Kennedy was a Catholic). I went to my bedroom and lay down, absolutely sickened by the thought of World War III and meeting God. I missed dinner that night, although I loved fried catfish at least as much as Doug did. I was a senior in high school at the time, but the war tarried long enough for me to start college. In college I ran into another guy who had the same level of concern about the imminence of WWIII, although not for supposed biblical reasons. We sat up many a night drawing out our plans to dig a very deep hole for a bomb shelter in an isolated field between our dorm and the women's dorm. We were going to fill it with food and water and build a secure hatch to protect us from the atomic bombs that were sure to come any day. Barksdale Air Force Base was the home of our B-52 bombers, and it was only seventy miles away.

One night I came into the dorm after a night of partying or gambling, both being high on my list of favorite pastimes, only to behold a shocking sight. The living room was absolutely full of guys watching the TV. I had never seen more than three or four nerdy guys in there at one time, my college being a party school. Our school mascot name was "Demons," so we had a reputation to uphold, and we did—except for this one night. As I joined the crowd, I quickly discovered that President Kennedy had initiated the Bay of Pigs invasion in Cuba. I was horror stricken. Gog and Magog were about to go at it and we didn't have our shelter dug! Once I became seriously religious and later began training for the ministry, the study of Doug's teaching, popularly known as premillennialism, became my passion. I was so happy to find out that all of the so-called end-time experts were twisting the Bible's teaching incredibly. It was true then with the Hal Lindsays of the world, and it is still true. The combination of my mother and Doug almost ruined my life of sin, at least for brief intervals. But false teaching, even given with the best of intentions, always makes you sick spiritually and sometimes physically.

Gordon on horseback...for adventure, yes this beats Xbox every time!

Atheism Failed Me

We often hear from atheists that humans invented the concept of God to comfort themselves when in trouble and when facing death. I rather think that they are 180 degrees off target. Most people would like to uninvent him, to rid themselves of the notion that they must have him as a Master and follow his laws or be damned. For sure, that is where I was at one point in my life. Until I went to college, I had never known an atheist personally. In the English department of my college, we had a husband-and-wife team who were both outspoken atheists, atheists with a vengeance. I wasn't offended by their comments; I was initially relieved. If there was no God, there was no Judge, and if there was no Judge, I didn't need to feel guilty any longer about my sinful lifestyle. In spite of being raised going to church every Sunday, I attended church one time in my college town in four years. I was busy partying and trying to become an atheist.

I discovered that it takes far more faith to be an atheist than a theist. I finally distilled my reasoning down to three points. No, not the questions, "Where did I come from? Where am I going? And what am I doing here?" Those are excellent questions, and my points were similar but not the same. First, I did have to deal with the origin issue, but for me it wasn't about where I came from but rather where *everything* came from. As far as I could tell, the Bible's first words were the right ones to start with: "In the beginning..." In the beginning, what? In the beginning, nothing became everything? Wow! In the beginning, rocks and dirt became all that we are and see? At least that way, you start with something, but where did the rocks and dirt come from in that theory? Genesis says, "In the beginning, God created..." Considering the available choices, what kind of idiot would it take to choose anything other than what Genesis says? As I said, atheism demands a faith far beyond anything I could conjure up.

During the Ferguson childhood, no animal was safe!

Then came the question of *why* he created man as the apex of all living creatures. He had to be more than a just Judge, or I would not have even been around to consider the questions. He would have annihilated mankind long ago, for all of us are rebels in one way or another. I planned to have children one day, as most people do, just because I love kids. That was the inescapable conclusion I reached about why God created us. He wanted us as his children. Finally, any parent who wanted children would long to communicate with them and rejoice when they spoke their first word—especially if it was "Mama" or "Dada." So how did God choose to communicate with us? Now the circle of logical reasoning was complete for me—back to the Bible, just like Mother said from my childhood. I could not escape that Book and the One who inspired it. The fact that atheism failed me didn't deter me from my life of sin, but deep down I always knew what was right and Who was right. I am glad I felt guilty all during those years—I deserved to, and at some point the guilt must have played some part in me starting to open up to God's advances. He is always in relentless and yet patient pursuit.

Gordon at high school graduation

When I spoke at my mother's funeral in January 2004, I shared with the audience three things that she loved and helped me to love: the Bible (eventually), characters (always) and children (also always). She had her problems emotionally and in her spiritual views of God and the Bible, but she never doubted the existence of God or the inspiration of the Bible. I learned other things from my dad for which I will always be thankful, namely the determination to be truthful (and expect it of others), the value of hard work (he was a construction guy) and a respect for authority. He later caught on spiritually, but it was my mother from birth who ultimately removed atheism as being a possibility for me and ingrained in me a belief in the Bible. It took someone else to help me love the Bible, but she gave me my faith in it. Thank you, Mom.

---

2. Lynn DeShazo, "Ancient Words" (Franklin, TN: Reunion Records, 2003).
3. John Melvin Henson, "Watching You" (Sacred Selections for the Church, #564).

Chapter Four

Thank God for the Bright Spots!

Well, by now I have painted a pretty dismal picture of my religious childhood, but it is a true picture. Had God not been in relentless pursuit of me, my future would have been pretty dismal too; I've no doubt of that. Most of the young people in the church of my youth (and there weren't that many) gave up on religion entirely. It's hard to blame them. I wanted to and nearly did. Along the way, there were a few positives, a few bright spots here and there. But make no mistake—the dim spots were far more numerous to me than the bright spots. Perhaps that's why they were high points, by comparison with the low ones.

Seeing Isn't Always Believing

Seeing reality doesn't always lead to spiritual belief. Someone once said that the world hasn't become Christian either because they've seen a Christian or because they haven't seen one. Although that sounds contradictory, it is an accurate statement, properly viewed. If they have seen a hypocrite, they are turned off; if they saw the real thing, a true Christian, they would be turned on. Most of those I saw in my church were of the first type. I knew them and I knew their lives. Many of them were my own relatives. However, our postman preacher was the real deal as far as his commitment to God was concerned. He believed it and he practiced it, and I suspect he preached it as best he could. To say that he didn't have the gift of teaching would be a kind way of putting it. Hence, my development of the art of daydreaming. But I never doubted his sincerity as a person trying to love and serve God. I felt sorry for him, but his example of trying so hard to be righteous was not totally lost on me. His sermons were, but not his example (a lesson all in itself). Although he always held the party line doctrinally, I always suspected that he didn't completely buy in. He seemed to grasp a bigger picture of God than the rest of us did.

After I left that church and eventually became part of a mainline Church of Christ, my path was destined to cross with his family's again years later. He had a fairly minor operation, and while he was still in the hospital recuperating, a blood clot hit his heart or lungs and killed him instantly. His widow decided to sell their house, although most grief experts say that we shouldn't make big decisions quickly after such a loss. My parents bought the house from her and lived there until my father died many years later. Our whole family loved that place. My children and nieces and nephews spent many days of their childhood playing in the huge backyard, shaded by towering pine and oak trees. I have many memories of family gatherings there, the last one being the fiftieth wedding anniversary of my parents just a few months before my dad died. Knowing that the house had belonged to a couple who served God to the best of their ability meant something to my parents and it meant something to me. That lone man was about the only example that had affected me to the extent he did.

Gordon (on the left) fishing for fish before he fished for men.

After I had become a minister in the mainline group, his widow contacted me through my mother. Her sister had died, and her husband approached our widow friend and put all his cards on the table. He had the same kind of heart that our former postman preacher had, and he was terribly lonely. Although he was some years older, he appealed to his sister-in-law to marry him while they still hopefully had some years left to live. Surprisingly, they asked me to perform the wedding ceremony, which I did. He lived for much longer than could have been expected, and they appeared to enjoy many happy years together. Somewhere in that mix was enough righteousness for God to bless them. I'm glad.

They were a bright spot to me when there weren't many others to see.

Christian Camp

I knew the brother-in-law just mentioned because of a Christian Camp facility on his property in a remote part of Louisiana. At least I think it was held on his property, or it could have been that he just ran the camp. Either way, those few summers I attended were the only times I ever remember having my heart affected spiritually in a serious way. It is said that politics make strange bedfellows. So do Christian Camps. Those who worked at the camp came from two different fellowships among the weird types: the one-cuppers and the premillennial group. Although our Texas friend Doug was premillennial in his views of the end times, no one at our little church knew enough about Revelation to know what those views were, as far as I could tell. But these two groups converged to conduct this teen camp each summer. Each time I attended, my heart was stirred temporarily, although I returned to my old ways immediately after camp ended and I came home.

The premillennial guys had the last name of Mullins. The dad, who was probably in his late sixties, was the nighttime preacher. He was a hellfire and brimstone type, but he could preach well enough to hold my attention when I was in my early and midteen years. It is often mentioned that teens have a short attention span, and admittedly, it is harder to keep the attention of those who are bombarded with so many forms of media compared to teens back in my day. But teens are bright minded and quick learners once they decide to listen. For whatever reason, I put my daydreaming habit away during teen camps and watched and listened carefully. I sat near the two younger Mullins men around the campfire at night as they conducted devotionals. They had good voices and were also good teachers like their dad. I don't remember one thing specifically that any of them taught, but I do remember their apparent sincerity and devotion. I look back at those camp weeks as the only real spiritual experiences of my growing-up years, and I'm thankful for them.

As a young teen, I was moved enough one night to get baptized in the swimming pool, along with a number of others. When I was in the car returning home from that camp session with my parents, my mother spotted my baptism certificate stuck in my Bible and asked about it. Since my parents had always been a part of my spiritually embarrassing experiences, their mere question was uncomfortable to me, and I briefly said I had been baptized and promptly changed the subject. Just writing this makes me sad, sad for me and sad for my parents. Many years later, I was rebaptized, knowing that my repentance had been all but absent when I was baptized initially. It was merely a fleeting emotional experience. My mother, especially, did the best she knew to do, but she just didn't know how to help a child (much less a teen) be spiritual. She tried a few things, but they had the opposite effect on me rather than what she had hoped for. Most of my feelings about those years from a spiritual perspective are just sad memories. Mom passed on all she knew to pass on, and when my kids were young, I passed on all I knew to pass on. I would give up almost anything I have for her to have known more and for me as a parent to have known more. I could have avoided hurting God, myself and my mother so much during my young years, and I could have helped my own family so much more than I did when I was the parent. Maybe that's why I teach and write—to help others do better, sooner.

Byrle and Violet Ferguson

It Ain't Over Till It's Over

That's poor grammar, but a wonderful concept to keep in mind. My dad died when I was a month shy of forty-nine years old. I was able to influence him spiritually in some very special ways after I became spiritually engaged. Mom died when I was sixty-one, and both she and Dad were able to hear me speak many, many times. I had persuaded them to leave their little church and become a part of the mainline group in our hometown that God used to change my life, which I will begin writing about in the next chapter. Their lives were changed there much as mine had been, as was my sister's. Bottom line, we all lived long enough to work through our religious past to get to better places. After studying with my parents, both were rebaptized in their later years. It's a marvel in many ways, but God made it happen for all of us. I spoke at both of their funerals and look back on our lives together with few regrets. They did their best, given their limitations, and kept growing. That's about all that we can ask of ourselves and of others.

From the standpoint of worldly fun, my childhood was marvelous. As a Louisiana kid, I spent much time in the outdoors fishing, hunting, camping and riding my horse. I had relatives who lived in the country and I loved staying with them as often as possible. I had many friends, although it is unfortunate that my influence on them was a sinful one. Theresa and I attended our fifty-year high school reunion several years back, mainly just to show them a different Gordon than the one they had known. I still communicate with a few of them from time to time, trying to have a spiritual influence on them in our late years. Only God knows what will become of those efforts.

As you can tell from this chapter, I have many regrets about my childhood from a spiritual perspective. I honestly was in a deep, dark hole spiritually until I was in my midtwenties, a story about to be told in the next section of the book. How I managed to crawl out of that hole when so many of my relatives and friends didn't is a miracle. I'm grateful to be out, and I give God all the credit for my escape. I'm just saddened in thinking about the many of those with whom I spent my youth who didn't have the same good fortune. Why God's behind-the-scenes pursuit of me ended up well, I haven't a clue—but I am most thankful. We all need to do more with those who are yet alive, don't you think? We cannot afford to waste our sin, for the memories of it have to do more than make us sad—they must motivate us to do all that we can to help others escape Satan's pit. So let's do it.

PART TWO:
THE MAINLINE CHURCH OF CHRIST AND MY LEGALISM

Chapter Five

My Baptist Wife and Religious Strife

Whether your background included time in the mainline Churches of Christ or not, you will learn some new and strange things. I need to preface what I say with some disclaimers or at least partial disclaimers. One, what I am writing in this entire book comes from my own memory banks, and as such, cannot be guaranteed to be one hundred percent accurate. No one's memory is perfect, and while mine is pretty amazing (to me, at least) on a long term basis, many of the details cannot be totally verified. Two, what I write is a combination of memories and perspectives. Even if the facts remembered are accurate, my own perception of those facts is colored by my own character and personality. All in all, I think that the large majority of those who shared these experiences or some very similar to them will agree that I am pretty accurate in both memory of the facts and my perception of those facts. If I were attempting to write a detailed history of the events covered, I would take the time to do more research. However, since I'm writing about my own spiritual history and perception thereof, I will continue telling my story as I recall it, believing that a reasonably high degree of accuracy is contained within.

I also need to mention that some of what I cover will have been covered in other writings of mine. For example, I included quite a bit of my spiritual history in another book just completed, *Fairy Tales Do Come True*.[4] This book is about our fifty-one-year marriage (as of January 30, 2016), which would never have achieved fairy tale status in our minds without the influence of our spiritual experiences. Thus, some overlap will occur from the marriage book and others, but I will work to keep it from being repetitious. Instead of just copying and dropping in material that is speaking of the same events or time periods, I will reference them from the other books, give an overall synopsis of them and add new details. The truth is that unless you read the material in both sources at about the same time, you likely wouldn't realize the similarities even if they were written exactly the same. However, I will approach these overlaps as I explained. Trust me on this: you will not get bored reading about the second stage of my religious experiences! It was quite a ride, with God in hot pursuit and stepping up the pace.

It's All My Wife's Fault!

Since the time of Adam and Eve, husbands have been far too quick to blame their wives for their own sins. In Genesis 3 when God started speaking to Adam about their sin of eating the forbidden fruit, Adam replied, *"The woman you put here with me—she gave me some fruit from the tree, and I ate it"* (verse 12). In my case, I am not blaming my wife for my spiritual turnaround, but giving her the credit and thanking her. The details of her influence on my church involvement are found in Chapter 5 of *Fairy Tales Do Come True*. The synopsis is that I hated going to church (not an overstatement) and she loved going to church. However, in a weak moment, I had somehow agreed prior to our wedding that I would attend the Baptist church with her and she would attend the Church of Christ with me, on an alternating basis. Maybe I agreed to attend every Sunday with her, which I certainly didn't do for at least a couple of years into our marriage. I suppose I wanted to get married so bad that I was willing to agree to a lot of things in order to persuade her to become Mrs. Ferguson.

I definitely wanted to marry Theresa from the time we fell in love as seniors in high school. We both wanted to attend and finish college, so I agreed to wait until we had graduated. However, I developed a secret dream of getting married while still in college and then graduating as husband and wife. My dad being a bricklayer led to me doing construction work every summer since getting out of the ninth grade and lasting through the summer after graduation from college. As a newlywed that last summer, and since I became a public school teacher, I needed the money. I saved up as much as I could through my college years in order to pay for most of my college costs, but I was also thinking about that dream of getting married before graduation.

The summer between my junior and senior years, my mother amazingly remembered a little insurance policy she had taken out for my education and presented me with it. Although it wasn't a large amount, in combination with my construction work savings, it allowed us to get married between our last two semesters in college. I mention those details to demonstrate that my desire to get married likely drove me to make some concessions to Theresa that were definitely not from the heart. Going to church, any church, was clearly in the concession category.

Ferguson Wedding Day - 1965

Since the church of my background was so weird and radically different from Theresa's Baptist experience, I decided that if I had to attend "my" church, it had better be a more traditional Church of Christ. Of course that was considered anathema to those in the church of my youth, but that mattered little to me. Hence, we visited the mainline types of congregations whenever Theresa successfully prevailed upon me to attend on any given Sunday. We only went to the Baptist church a couple of times, as I recall, and I couldn't handle their teaching and practices regarding the conversion process. I may not have known much Bible at the time, but I knew enough about the conversion passages to know that their standard evangelical approach was clearly wrong. I soon refused to attend "her" church with her, and she wanted to go somewhere enough that she agreed to just attend my church. That was nothing like a victory for me—quite the opposite. I was hoping to escape attending anywhere. But alas, what could I do with her offer besides start attending with some degree of frequency, about every third week? The intervening weeks I spent Sundays doing what I wanted to be doing every Sunday, namely fishing or hunting.

When we did attend church, we had about five or six congregations in our city from which to choose. We tried them all, and all of them seemed about the same to me. The people were nice, too nice for me to be comfortable in their midst, given my worldly lifestyle at the time. The preachers were boring and otherworldly to me; they certainly were no part of my world and when they mentioned my world, it was only to condemn it (with biblical accuracy, admittedly). For a couple of years, we attended occasionally, but mainly focused on trying to achieve the American Dream.

In Hot Pursuit of the American Dream

Both of us started our careers as teachers. I was a musician and band director, first at the junior high school level and then the high school level. As a musician, I also played a lot of gigs to earn extra money, plus it was who I was at that time and I loved doing it. I also taught a number of private students in my home to make even more money. Theresa taught sixth grade in the same elementary school that she and her brothers had attended growing up, plus she too had a couple of part-time jobs, mostly in selling educational materials. Together, we made enough money to buy a pretty good chunk of that American Dream, including our first and second homes (moving up, you know), two cars, a fishing boat, a camper, a fishing camp with my dad and five acres of land in a restricted subdivision on which to build our dream home (which we never built). The fishing camp played a significant role in the direction of my life, very unexpectedly. I loved that camp, as did my father, and we spent many days fishing from it, often with each other and separately with other friends at times.

One beautiful summer day, I had fished with a friend, who had driven down separately for some reason. We caught the limit of largemouth bass, my favorite type to fish for, and then my friend left. I stayed around for a while, since it was such a beautiful day and the lake view was simply spectacular from the end of our pier. Life was good, good indeed. Here I was at age twenty-five with lots of possessions and adult toys, a beautiful wife and a new baby boy and a very successful career. What could be better? As I was standing on my pier, beside my turquoise bass boat, a thought came from out of nowhere (from God, in retrospect) and hit me like a ton of bricks. "Is this all there is to life? I'm a quarter-century old, having achieved so much so fast, but what's next? Do you just keep doing all of this until you get old and die? Is that it?"

God's Invasion(s)

Those scary thoughts didn't just come out of nowhere. They came from Theresa's increasing effectiveness at getting me to church and the spiritual truths that were starting to take root somewhere deep down in my soul. God has many ways to invade our psyches, and he is relentless in his pursuit of us. I remember a dear sister in San Diego describing her conversion in a small-group setting, and she said that she wasn't looking for God at all, but he invaded her anyway. That to me is a rather magical way to describe God's providence in our lives as he leads us to himself. I almost used some form of that statement as a title of this book. God has openly invaded my life countless times, in some large, obvious ways and in some small, subtle ways. But, praise his name, he is a pursuer and invader of souls!

By the time I was standing on that fishing-camp pier, we were going to one particular congregation regularly and were pretty involved. I didn't recognize it at the time, but that series of disturbing questions that flooded my soul was actually my first call to preach. The emptiness of the world, at its best, was still emptiness. Nothing can fill the void created in us except the One who created both us and the void. I had to learn that the hard way, but I am so thankful God helped me to learn it at such a young age. Many don't learn it at all and many learn it only when they are old and facing death. I learned it at age twenty-five. I still had a lot to work through and out of at that point, but I was never the same after that fateful day. Thank you, Jesus!

It was probably not too long before that time that the preacher for our congregation had been used by God to invade me. Knowing God much better now, it is no surprise that he used my love of fishing as his entry point. In that same chapter of my marriage book, Chapter 5, I tell the story of how all of that occurred. The material there came from a book long out of print, *Discipling*, but it is a story worth telling. You can read the details of it in the other book if you want to (and I hope you will). Interestingly, many years later this preacher, Richard Hostetler, shared with me the story of his conversion, and it came at the hands of another preacher I met in more recent years named Jim Woodruff. My preacher friend died some years back, but Jim might still be alive. I met him in 2004 at an event I will mention later, and had read at least two of the books he authored prior to that time. Richard simply practiced discipling, even if he wouldn't have recognized it by that term, passing on to me what he had learned from Jim. They both used fishing for fish as an aid to fishing for men. Striking! Richard had been just as big a sinful mess when he started fishing with Jim as I was when I started fishing with Richard. In both cases, it was an invasion by God, clearly (and thankfully).

I do urge you to go back and read that chapter from the marriage book. When I stated above that I had much to work through and out of when I was first called to preach, you will have little idea of what a formidable task that was without knowing more of the details. Assuming that you have read the first four chapters of this book, you know what my weird religious background was and how it affected me. But being invaded and reprogrammed by God was a very gradual and painful process in many ways, especially in those early days of our marriage and joint spiritual experiences. One of the most painful experiences was trying to overcome my extreme timidity when speaking in public. Those who didn't know me back in those days find it nearly impossible to believe the extent of my fears of public speaking. There were many other obstacles to get over and around, but this one was like scaling a mountain for me. You can read the details of that period in one of my earliest books (the crowd favorite, by the way), *The Victory of Surrender,* in the chapter entitled "Surrender: The Only Path to Security." With that, you have the story of my introduction to the second stage of my religious life, the mainline church stage, and that stage was ushered in by a wife and strife! God works in mysterious ways, then, now and always.

---

4. *Fairy Tales Do Come True,* Gordon Ferguson, Illumination Publishers, Spring, Texas, 2016. Available at www.ipibooks.com

Chapter Six

Amazing Breakthroughs

Characters Welcome

I introduced this concept when talking about my mother in Chapter 3. As I am a character and love characters, it won't come as a surprise that my preacher friend Richard, although he had many engaging qualities, was indeed a character. When we first went fishing together, with me topping out the apprehensive scale, it didn't take long to make this discovery. He introduced me to a special fishing tradition of his. On every fishing trip, when he caught his first fish, he took it off the hook, stared at it gleefully for about five seconds and then with some sort of yell, put the fish's head in his mouth and bit it. When he did it on that first trip, I almost jumped out of my skin (it was a really loud yell). For a brief moment, I thought maybe I was not only stuck in a boat as a captive audience to a preacher, but maybe a crazy preacher. We once took a rather reserved elder in our church fishing, and when Richard caught his first fish, I knew what was coming, but Clay had no idea. I watched his face carefully as Richard kept his tradition intact, and would give a lot of money for a picture of Clay's face when Richard did his thing. If we hadn't caught another fish, that moment would have been more than worth the cost of time and money spent.

Richard Hostetler

Richard did have a very winsome side. When someone came into his office for some counseling help and sat down, he would get this tender look on his face, tilt his head slightly to one side, and ask softly, "How can I help?" I've definitely imitated that type of approach to put people at ease. Since Richard was six foot, five inches tall and weighed about 260, he needed some ways to help minimize the intimidation factor. He also had a great sense of humor and laughed a lot. In our town, the Church of Christ had quite a reputation among religious folks. They were known for what they didn't have, especially instrumental music in worship. But the most negative view of this movement was often expressed this way when you shared your church affiliation: "Oh, you're the ones that think everyone is going to hell except those in your denomination!" That reputation lives on even today, with older people especially. At any rate, Richard had a unique response to comments like that one. He laughed loudly and said, "To tell you the truth, I think about eighty percent of them aren't going to make it either!" I might be wrong on the percentage he used, but it was something close to that. The comment certainly diffused the tension in the ones who heard it. Richard said it as a joke, but he wasn't totally joking, based on the sermons on total commitment I heard him preach. He had a wonderful balance in his preaching of total commitment, evangelism and the grace of God. It changed my heart and life, and later, that of my parents, and has helped me through the years to strive for a balanced diet that leads to spiritual health.

My one-cup background was legalistic to the core. My first ministry training was certainly bent in the legalistic direction. The Church of Christ in general in those days was bent the same way. Of course, that doesn't mean that every member in the mainline group had that mindset, but in general, most did. Richard didn't, thankfully. He came out of a Baptist background, but responded about the same as I had to my background—with rebellion and sin. He was kicked out of his last public school when in the ninth grade. The principal of his school called him into the office, along with his mother, and was about to lay down the law about Richard's behavior when Richard calmly took out a cigarette and lit it up right there. That act of defiance ended his public-school career. He must have taken a GED course or something similar to show that he had graduated high school, because he later attended Harding College (now University) and graduated. Evidently when Jim introduced him to Christ, Richard must have not only accepted the conversion process but also reclaimed the good part of his Baptist roots, namely loving Jesus. His faith reminded me a lot of Theresa's, whose picture of Jesus in her mind is one with him surrounded by sheep and little children.

My First Mainline Experience Was a Good One

With my description of Richard in mind, you understand the heading of this section. I didn't know any Bible, but Richard loved the Bible and talked about it as naturally as others talk about sports and weather. A day fishing with him was like attending a Bible class, except it was so natural and exciting that all of my resistance to spiritual things was taken away pretty quickly after we started fishing together. That is pretty amazing, since I was still very much in the world at the time, drinking, smoking, cursing and the like. When I started allowing God to extricate me from these unsavory habits, I asked Richard to help me start learning the Bible. I knew very little about it. He had me start reading certain books in the Bible and told me to write down my questions about what I didn't understand. Then I would go up to his office, ask my questions and get the answers. Richard knew his Bible well. As we continued the process, I learned quickly and usually figured out most of the answers to my questions myself. But I still went to his office to bounce my findings off of him.

He also played some tapes of sermons from other preachers for me, most of whom were not in the Church of Christ. I still remember two sermons he played by Robert G. Lee, an old Baptist preacher of the last century. One was entitled "Payday Someday," and the other "Christ Above All." When I heard that second one in Richard's office, I was left so emotionally high that I felt like I was floating and would have to push myself down from the ceiling to get through the doors. The first of those sermons is available on YouTube at the time of this writing, and both are on http://www.goodpreachin.com/. I transcribed both of them in my early preaching days and have preached them both (but not as well as R.G. Lee did). I've recommended listening to those lessons to others, some of whom couldn't understand his old Southern accent. It's much stronger than mine, if you can believe that!

Richard lit my flame spiritually in many ways, by God's grace.

The changes that were taking place in my heart were pretty much unbelievable, even to me. I was such a pagan in mindset and lifestyle prior to Richard that I often said that he was probably the only preacher in the whole state of Louisiana who could have gotten to me, which meant that he had been sent specially for me. I started crying while writing these words, because I believe those two things are actually true. He only stayed in the preaching business a few years, but those were my years and God's years for me. Amazing grace, how sweet the sound! God's pursuit continued, picking up still more speed as it did.

Our congregation was rather unique among those in the city. Most of the other congregations viewed us as "liberal," which in retrospect was a good thing. As much as I had grown to love Richard's preaching, his continued emphasis on God's grace being able to enable us to do anything had frustrated me greatly. I just didn't believe that type of assertion applied to everyone, least of all me. Hence, one night after an evening service I told a deacon in the church that I was going to pull out all of the stops for a year and do anything I was asked to do, but if it didn't work like Richard said, then I was done with church. The deacon, Robbie, just smiled softly and said gently, "Sounds like a good plan to me." Of course that year has never ended. Robbie was a man of wisdom and real spirituality. At some point, the church bought some nearby property and built group homes for orphaned children. Robbie and his wife were the first set of house parents for the first of several such large homes. As I said, it was a unique congregation, with more than the usual share of people who were also taking Richard's teaching to heart.

Evangelism and Campaigns

It wouldn't surprise you to know that this congregation was much more evangelistic than most in that day. I went on my first personal study with Robbie, and on others with Richard. Evangelistic campaigns were in vogue for a number of years back then. They may well have had their genesis in watching what Billy Graham was doing in his campaigns. In the mainline churches, we had printed materials about the upcoming campaign to pass out, along with the invitation to study the Bible in their homes right then. I remember Theresa knocking doors when she was obviously quite pregnant. We loved knocking those doors and studying with people. It was never a burden to us but a special privilege. Under Richard's leadership, nothing was a burden. I dedicated a whole chapter in the marriage book to financial giving (Chapter 7), because once I opened my mind and heart to what he taught, giving changed our lives and our marriage.

When the actual preaching campaign took place, it was in a very large, well-known rented facility, and the preaching was done by guest preachers known to be effective with large crowds. Two names that come to mind as campaign speakers in those days are Mid McKnight and Jimmy Allen. Jimmy taught at Harding College, and his son, Jimmy Allen, Jr. is one of the evangelist/elders in our movement and leads a church in Providence, Rhode Island. Hundreds of visitors attended those campaigns, which usually lasted for several nights, and many were baptized. One version of the campaign approach added a five-night TV show, with live call-in Bible questions answered by a live panel. This addition took place either before or after the public preaching segment. I don't remember which, although as a fledgling preacher I was on one of the live panels once or twice and was the speaker for the public meeting once. I will say more about that a bit later in the book.

Southern Hills Church of Christ where Gordon got headed in the right direction.

When our son was a baby, which would have made me about twenty-five years old, at Richard's urging we attended a personal evangelism workshop at Harding College in Searcy, Arkansas (his alma mater). Within the mainline churches at that time, certain men had become known for their effectiveness at converting people and being able to preach powerfully about it. Theresa and I left Bryan with my parents and attended that several-day event during the Thanksgiving holidays. We met people whose books we had read and whose names we had heard. Riding on an elevator with them left us awestruck and starstruck. The Harding Fall Lectureship was taking place concurrently, and we left our meeting once to hear Jimmy Allen preach a sermon on grace at the lectureship. I still remember the lesson, for Jimmy was a powerful speaker and it was a wonderful lesson. We drove back to Louisiana after it was over, fully convinced that we wanted to figure out how to go into the ministry. It was a mountaintop experience for which we will ever be grateful. With Richard's emphasis on both grace and evangelism, it was no wonder that both would fit into my future in a number of significant ways.

Legalism Postponed and Diluted

This second part of the book, describing my experiences in the mainline Church of Christ, has as part of the title, "My Legalism." With my one-cup background and the general tenor of the mainline in the days of my youth, legalism was inescapable. That being said, for me it was postponed for a time and actually diluted forever, all due to Richard's influence. Long after he was no longer preaching, he was living in Oklahoma City and working in the oil business (quite successfully). Although we didn't stay in close touch during the latter part of his life, we did talk or write some. He knew of the Discipling Movement (by whatever name) only by reputation, but he knew me and remained quite proud of me all of his life. When I started writing books, he would buy them and give them to others. Once I spoke at our sister church in Oklahoma City and persuaded him to come and hear me and then go out to lunch together. I explained to that small audience who he was and how much of an influence he had been in my life. I further explained that I was going to speak my sermon directly to him, but they were more than welcome to listen in. That comment got a laugh from the audience, but I wasn't kidding. I went back to the days when God used him to change my life and reminded him of his own three main emphases in preaching. I told him that I ended up in this present movement precisely because of his teaching, since it was the only group I had discovered that actually taught the same things. It was quite a moment for the two of us, and we had a great lunch afterward. I never did persuade him to join our group, but he knew what we were about and liked much of what he knew.

I feel compelled to mention at least three things as I end this chapter. One, I know that we in the Discipling Movement have had (and some still have) our own brand of legalism. We have done much repenting and changing, but many of us have not yet completely escaped the clutches of legalism. Some who have escaped have gone to the opposite extreme and

The Ferguson family (with newborn Byran) were ready to transition into ministry.

are little different from evangelicals in their thinking. They don't exalt doctrinal truthfulness, but now they minimize it, which is still a sin. Two, there were many exceptions to a legalistic mindset in the mainline churches in the earlier days. I read books and heard sermons from mainline preachers that helped me tremendously in the direction of grace, and I have used their material until this very day. Three, I can't speak to where things are in the mainline group with any degree of authority, since I left that fellowship thirty-one years ago. In more recent years, I have spoken a few times in mainline church settings for one event or another and have been received quite warmly. Bridges once burned down have been rebuilt, which is encouraging. However, the reasons for which I left still remain in that group as far as I can tell, but I didn't leave because of their legalism at the time. I will explain exactly why I left in more detail later in the book. I just felt compelled to clarify a few things in this present chapter before we end it. Done. On to the next chapter...

Chapter Seven

Ministry Training as Student and Teacher

Up until now, I likely haven't ruffled anyone's feathers. In Part One (my first religious life), I was talking about my experiences long ago in the one-cup, no-Sunday-school group of churches. I can't imagine anyone from that background (if they still even exist as a movement) reading this book. Just about everyone I knew in that setting is dead and gone. That reminds me of a joke I heard that relates, at least in one sense. A certain preacher was preaching about loving our enemies, praying for them and doing good toward them. At some point in the sermon, he said, "Is there anyone present who can truthfully say that you have no enemies?" One really old guy in the back, at least ninety years of age, raised his hand. The minister was a bit shocked, but thrilled. He asked the old guy to come forward to the microphone, and handed it to him. He then requested that the old fellow please share with the group how he reached the hallowed state of having no enemies. He spoke into the microphone clearly and loudly, "I've outlived all those #%*+*&#@!"

As I began Part Two about my mainline church experiences, I've only said negative things about me in my overtly sinful pagan state. Now I am about to enter the parts that could ruffle some feathers, and that will continue when I discuss the movement of which I am a part at present. One's history is one's history, and humans are imperfect at best. Hence, if I am to be honest about what I experienced and believed (or still believe), it has to include the good, bad and ugly. God wrote the Bible in that way; but of course, he is infallible, unlike me, and yet I have to paint the full picture as best I can.

When I first started outlining this second part about my life in the mainline group, I was thinking of leaving out some things. Then I started thinking about why I might do that. I think it traces back to a concept and some actual experiences. The concept is that sometimes we don't think an "outsider" to a situation has any right to share negative aspects about people or movements. It's like someone saying, "I can say those things about my mama, but you can't!" I think the experiences go back to certain mainline leaders attending some of "our" events and being supersensitive about some of our in-house wording (although they may have been technically correct about their objections). I think of one former college Bible teacher who fit into that category, and yet he wrote books about the mainline church that were far more negative about his own group than anything I'm going to write in this book. So, you have fair warning not to take things personally. Besides, the experiences I will write about took place when I was a full-fledged member of the mainline church. I paid my dues and earned the right to speak as a then-insider. If your experiences and opinions are different from mine in some areas that I disliked, be thankful. This is still a country that technically espouses free speech (though the Politically Correct Enforcement Corps have nearly destroyed it for any who see things differently from them). I intend to use my constitutional right to free speech, because it is also a God-given right. I'll try hard to be sensitive and evenhanded in the process, OK?

After my visit to Harding College, I was ready to get more training and preach.

After the Divine Call, What's Next?

As I mentioned in the last chapter, Theresa and I came back from that event at Harding College having been bitten by the ministry bug—hard! After that, I couldn't think of much else. My career started crumbling so badly that one of my fellow teachers from the high school where we both taught called Richard and encouraged him to help find a way to put me out of my misery (and into the pulpit). My misery was that obvious even to a teacher that I didn't know that well.

At this point, I had an undergraduate degree in music education and about half of a master's degree in supervision and administration at the secondary level. I knew if I stayed in teaching, I would become a principal, so I was working toward that degree. With my new yearning, I assumed that if I wanted to become a minister I would have to start over at the undergraduate level to get Bible training, but I had a wife and child to support. I had no answers to my dilemma.

Richard said that perhaps I could get into a graduate school of theology, so I began looking into that. One winter day, we drove on icy roads to Memphis and back the same day, slipping and sliding all the way. We spoke with an administrator at what was then known as Harding Graduate School of Religion (now Harding School of Theology). The best suggestion he could come up with was for me to use my educational training and take enough courses to become what was called an educational director for a church. He thought I could work for a church part time or get another type of part-time job and Theresa might get a job as well. Although it didn't sound overly enticing to me, because I really wanted to preach, it seemed to be a step in the right direction, so I pursued it further. Richard was sure that he could find me some financial help, particularly from a rich guy he knew who supported ministry training efforts. Thus, I was seemingly at the brink of seeing my dream come true. That turned out to be a very brief period of elation.

I will never forget the look on Richard's face when he came to tell me that the rich guy wouldn't give me the money. He had a policy that he only helped men get their basic Bible training, not graduate training. I will also never forget the pain that came into my heart with that pronouncement—it was a knife to the heart, yielded by God himself. I never thought to blame my friend who almost promised the support or his friend who turned down my support. From the start, I knew this was all about God and me, not me and men. Job became my Bible book of choice during many late-night sessions, after Theresa and Bryan were asleep. My face was drenched with tears and a thousand "Whys?" were directed at God. "Why did you create this desire in me and then slam the door in my face?"; "Why am I not good enough to serve you in this way?"; "Why didn't you somehow persuade the rich man to alter his policy at Richard's urging?"; "I have said with Isaiah, 'Here am I, send me' and why have you just said no, with no explanation at all?" As I said, long nights, long prayers, long sorrow—for about two years. There was no one to be angry at except God, and so we had our own little private battleground in my living room, kept private in order not to hurt anyone else's faith, especially that of my little wife.

A Fateful Phone Call

Do you believe in destiny? People often ask that question. If you believe in God and you read the Bible, you cannot possibly believe otherwise, if his providence is determining that destiny. As Paul was helping kill Christians, his destiny was nonetheless set in the opposite direction. In Galatians 1:15 he said, *"God...set me apart from my mother's womb"* to be what he became. One day Richard and I were eating fish for lunch (since we loved eating them about as much as we loved catching them) while Theresa was teaching school. As we were eating, Richard mentioned that he had met a preacher in southern Louisiana who had attended a different kind of ministry training school than he had any familiarity with, but said that the guy was a good preacher. He suggested that we go over to the church office after lunch and call the man to get more information. Richard knew what was still in my heart and he still believed God had a plan for my destiny. (By then, I didn't.)

We made the call, and the preacher to whom we spoke gave me the name of the school, described how it functioned, and left me with the phone number of the school and the name of its director. Richard said, "Why don't you just call the school and ask for a brochure?" I called and told the secretary who answered what I wanted. The next thing I knew, the director was on the line asking me questions about myself, and I kept saying that I just wanted a brochure. Before the conversation was over, he said that he was flying over in his private plane the next day to talk to me about coming to the school immediately, since the new semester had just started that very day. I thought I had somehow fallen into the *Twilight Zone*. Was this guy crazy or something? I was in a daze when I got off the phone, and about twenty minutes after I drove home, Richard called to say that the crazy director had called back and talked to him further about me and was now on his way to the airport to fly the two hours over to see me. He wanted to have dinner with us and then spend the night. I just stared at the phone, wondering what kind of dream this was. I had called for a brochure and now some unknown guy was flying over to meet us and spend the night with us. I kept waiting to wake up from this dream or nightmare or whatever it was.

I picked Theresa up at school about 3:30 that afternoon, and started out something like, "Honey, I've got something to tell you that is more than a little crazy..." She started planning dinner on the way home, and as she cooked it, I went to the airport to pick up a man in a suit carrying two briefcases as he ran across the tarmac. As we drove home, we started getting acquainted a bit, and he started telling me about the school. It was called a school of preaching and was designed to train as ministers those who were usually beyond college age but wanted to go into the ministry. Since the new semester had started that same day, almost from the beginning he was saying that I should come to Dallas that upcoming Sunday and start school Monday, only one week late. Here I was, a married man with a little boy, a mortgage and no money to go to school. None of that seemed to faze him. He informed me that a student had dropped out that day and that one of the congregations in my town had been giving him some support, so he got on the telephone to call one of the elders of that congregation to invite him over to my house right then. Then Richard appeared at my door unexpectedly, informing me that he had called his rich friend again and the sort of program I was considering would fit within his policy parameters, so I could count on some support from him after all.

From there on, it was all pretty much a blur. About midnight, the director (who was either crazy or just a true zealot) looked at me and said, "OK—what about it? Are you coming?" I looked at him for a few moments, felt the Holy Spirit's presence without doubt, and said simply, "Yes." He had done quite a sales job, but he must have wondered if he had oversold me, for he said rather tentatively, "Are you sure?" I replied in the affirmative again. He

Eldred Stevens and wife. Eldred was the director of the Preston Road School of Preaching.

turned to Theresa and asked her what she was thinking about it all. She said, "Gordon has been absolutely miserable for the last couple of years, wanting to preach so bad he could taste it, so if this is not the answer, I don't know what else could be." Eldred (the director) spent the rest of a short night and flew home early the next morning. We had a house to sell in a week or two, with four or five others already up for sale on our block (ours sold in one week *just* because our next-door neighbors had close friends who wanted to live close to them). We had jobs to leave, family to tell and then leave, and a church full of friends to say goodbye to—in less than a week. I drove to Dallas on that upcoming Sunday, started school the next day, drove back to my hometown 200 miles away on Friday night to pick up my wife and child and a truck full of our belongings that my dad and uncles had loaded, and we drove back to Dallas the next morning. The two years in that school, studying around the clock pretty much, seven days a week, were like heaven to me. My two years of misery had been divinely ended in just less than twelve hours. Do I believe in destiny? What do you think?! If you don't, keep reading.

A Different Kind of Training

During my second year of attending the Preston Road School of Preaching, we moved out to the little town (now a suburb) of Cedar Hill. They needed someone to lead their teen ministry and were willing to help us out with a small amount financially in return for that service. We lived in a little country house and had a memorable year in many ways. The teen ministry was a mess, but we made many friends and did the best we could on such a part-time basis. We did have one full summer there and were able to do much more then. After the summer was over, graduation was only four months away. What was I going to do after that? I had no idea about how to go about finding a job, but I prayed that God had a plan. Doesn't he always? The route to God's plan for the next chapter in my life was circuitous, to say the least.

Prior to being offered the job at Cedar Hill, I had gone to speak at a fairly large congregation in the Dallas area and also interview for the same type of teen-ministry role with them. I knew the minister there (not well), who later taught me at the school of preaching. Everything seemed to go quite well that Sunday, but they called a couple of days later to say that they wanted to hire someone with more time before graduation, since I had less than a year to go. That was very disappointing, but understandable, and then God opened the door at Cedar Hill. The important piece of the puzzle is that this other minister where I didn't go (my future teacher) heard me speak and got to know me better. That was all a part of this destiny thing.

In the meantime, a former minister in the Fort Worth area named J.T. Bristow had moved to Vancouver, Washington to work for a church there, or actually have that congregation as a home base from which to launch a new program called Outreach. He was one of those speakers at the personal evangelism workshop at Harding College that we had heard some years back and had conducted a wide-scale campaign in the Dallas-Ft. Worth area called Impact Christ. He moved to the Northwest to develop more materials for personal evangelism and to conduct weekend motivational workshops to promote personal evangelism. He had at one time been a motivational speaker in nonreligious settings, being quite a speaker. The problem that developed in his ministry was that it grew too fast for him to keep up with, and he needed another person to join him in holding these workshops. However, the church couldn't afford another experienced guy like him, so he was looking for someone inexperienced with potential who could work for much less money. He contacted the other preacher in

O. J. Russell reccommended me to J. T. Bristow which led me to Vancouver.

Dallas who had met me (O.J. Russell was his name), and asked him if he had any suggestions. Bingo! O.J. recommended that they interview me. In October 1971, two months before graduation, Theresa and I flew on our first jet airplane to Portland (just across the river from Vancouver). I preached and interviewed and was hired, all in one weekend. In early January, we headed out to live away from the South for the first time.

Once in Vancouver, J.T. started training me. We talked a lot, evangelized by knocking doors during the weeks, and I accompanied him to the workshops he was holding. They consisted of a Sunday school teaching session, a morning motivational sermon (*really* motivational), a two-hour afternoon teaching session about how to set up studies with people and then study with them, and an evening motivational sermon. I learned very quickly that this guy was one of the most motivational speakers I had ever heard. As a result, I realized just as quickly that if I didn't catch on really fast and improve equally fast, those who called for workshop appointments were going to say, "Send J.T., not that new young guy." So, we were thousands of miles from where home had always been for us, in a new congregation where we knew no one initially, and in a pressure-cooker of a role. I had preached some at small churches as a fill-in while in school, but I had little experience doing the kind of preaching and teaching that J.T. did.

J. T. Bristow and sons on the farm in Washington state

Thankfully, he was a willing teacher and a genuine character. We became good friends quickly and remained so for the rest of his life. Cassette-tape recorders were fairly new at the time, but I had one. I taped everything he did, transcribed it, and changed nothing unless an illustration couldn't be stretched to fit me. In other words, I immediately embraced the fine art of imitation.

It wasn't rocket science—this guy could preach much better than I could, but I had his material and heard him enough in person and on tape to do what he did just about as well as he did it. He started having me preach or teach different parts of the workshop, with him in the audience. I didn't think it strange to try to duplicate exactly what he did, down to the finest details, and he didn't think it strange. It was truly amazing how quickly I was able to preach just like him and just as effectively. I can't say that all of my sermons outside the workshop setting were as good as those I stole from him, but I grew rapidly in my abilities to speak. I was as amazed as anyone, but the harsh realities of life (like my job being on the line) provide the best motivation possible. It was a marvelous experience, and we grew to love the Northwest and that congregation. We had no shortage of friends and fun after a fairly brief transition. Our daughter was born there within a few months of our move. It became home quickly, which meant that the adaptability factor so vital to someone in ministry had grown at a rapid rate as well.

J. T. Bristow on his farm in Washington

It's all rather amazing, looking back at it. God was not just relentless in his pursuit of me in the early days; he is very much still at it. Further, he is not just relentless in pursuit of having a relationship with me, but equally relentless in his pursuit of carrying out his plan for me. Do you believe that's also true of God and you? I pray that you do, because it is unquestionably true. I'm nothing special compared to anyone reading this book. God is after you

Gordon in the Northwest...we were all young once!

Outreach *paper begun by J. T. to promote evangelism and the work being done in the Northwest*

just as much as he is after me, and he has a detailed plan for you just as much as he has one for me. You desperately need to believe that, open up your heart fully to him, look for his plan and embrace it. Yes, this book contains the life story of one person, but your life story means as much to God as mine does. Live it out and live it to the full. The only limits for any of us are the ones we set, not the ones he sets. If you believe that, rejoice and get on with allowing him to write the rest of your story. If you have a hard time believing it, borrow my faith for a while and invite him to help you surrender. Wild adventures lie ahead—and with that, we are off to the next chapter of the book (and of our lives).

Chapter Eight

Wild Adventures—Almost Too Young and Too Soon

Actually, as I write all of this ministry life history down, something is dawning on me. From the time I first made that vow to Robbie (to go all out and be all in), a pattern started developing that I believe has lasted for decades. God is not only totally unpredictable in how he chooses to work in our lives; he is totally adventuresome. He loves surprising us. He loves forcing us out of our small-thinking boxes and narrow comfort zones. He knows how much we can handle, and he pushes us right to that limit. He recognized me as having a fond appreciation of adventure and a large capacity to endure it. I've done a lot of really crazy things through the years, enough to have already outlined a weird humor book that won't require much embellishment at all. I've lived it from youth; the title of this chapter encapsulates the concept. God made me and understands me. He knows that I like adventure and quickly get bored with the more mundane aspects of life. I've often described my life with God as him jumping unexpectedly out from behind bushes and scaring me half to death. The key word in the chapter title is "almost." Many adventures in ministry came my way almost too soon when I was almost too young. I will pick up where the last chapter left off and you will see what I mean. The transition from student to teacher to student to teacher has been a cyclical experience.

Another Fateful Phone Call

In early January of 1970, I made that fateful phone call that ended up with Eldred Stevens on the other end, him in my house only a few hours later, and me enrolled in his school in another few hours. In the fall of 1973, I was on the receiving end of another fateful phone call, this one placed by Eldred to me. It was almost as shocking and scary as first one. Just prior to my graduation from the Preston Road school, I had what I think was called a senior conference with the faculty of the school. I had been an outstanding student, making almost all A's in the most difficult school I had (or have) ever attended (by quite a margin). I had some gifts in the teaching arena, and an educational background as well. Hence, the faculty was quite complimentary of the work I had done, and to my amazement, they expressed a desire to have me back one day as a member of the faculty. I had just turned twenty-nine, and I assumed that any invitation to return as a teacher would be at least a decade away, after I had gained a sufficient amount of ministry experience.

The phone call from Eldred was an invitation to come back then, just over two years from my graduation. I honestly thought to myself that he had lost at least part of his mind. To come back then would mean that I was the first graduate to be invited back to be a part of the faculty and that I would be the youngest teacher they had ever had and the only one without at least a master's degree. What were they thinking? I asked him exactly that question—what in the world were they thinking? He explained that although their present faculty members were experienced in ministry and in teaching, the school needed an evangelistic emphasis that they believed I could provide. Under J.T.'s tutelage, I had grown fast and gained much experience in the field of evangelism, both personally and publicly. I had conducted workshops in a number of different places in the Northwest and in other states as well. Somehow the reputation had spread that I was really good in the area of evangelism. Honestly, that was a hard phone call for me to digest. It was highly flattering, to be sure, but overwhelming at the same time. When in school training, my teachers were my heroes. The idea of becoming their peer was nigh impossible to get my head around. Besides that, J.T. had put a lot of himself into me, and leaving would surely hurt him and very possibly leave the impression that I neither understood nor appreciated what he had done for me. It was a gut-wrenching time. I liked what I was doing and had become good at it, more than good perhaps. At that very time, I was set to travel to Texas to raise support for the Outreach ministry. I felt conflicted; I felt like a hypocrite as I did my fund-raising. *Almost* too young to be doing what I was doing anyway, and *almost* too soon to consider the offer for another adventure? Absolutely—almost.

A Definite Pattern

Almost too young and almost too soon—a definite pattern. It started in my home congregation in Shreveport. As a father of a very young son, I was asked to serve as a deacon in the church—too young and too soon. That was one of my shocks, but I agreed. After all, I had vowed to Robbie Mitchell not to refuse any spiritually based request that came my way. That time I was too young as a father to have demonstrated enough parenting skills, based on 1 Timothy 3:12, but I seemed to do well in that role nonetheless. I wasn't too young to attend preaching school, but it was almost too soon, given my abysmal lack of Bible knowledge upon entering. I felt like a lion in a den full of Daniels. I caught up to where most of the students were fairly soon, but I slept little and studied much for some months. The first semester I was almost done in by the amount of material to be learned, almost all of which was foreign to me, plus all of the verses to be memorized. But within a couple of months, I discovered that minds are like muscles. They weaken fast with disuse and strengthen fast with use. My mind became like a firm muscle within a short time, and I was amazed at how fast and how much I was capable of learning. Honestly, I had been a party boy all the way through my previous education, smart enough to get by without much focus, and I first realized my intellectual capabilities while in preaching school. Thus, entry into that program was almost too soon, but not quite.

Next came the Vancouver chapter of my training and ministry. As already described, my work with Outreach definitely came *almost* too soon when I was almost too young as far as ministry experience went. But much, much more happened in Vancouver outside of Outreach. We had a publication by the name of *Outreach*, and I was of course a writer for that, something of a new experience for me. The Northwest was known as the most unchurched area in the country, and not only were the Churches of Christ few and far between, but most of them were small. I soon became a big fish in a very small pond and consequently received many invitations to speak. J. T. led Impact for Christ campaigns both years I was there, and I was asked to serve on the live TV panel mentioned earlier. Our first year in the campaign, we brought in Jimmy Allen as the guest speaker. He did his usual great job and we baptized a number of people. J.T. and I spent a whole day with him showing him the Columbia River Gorge and talking Bible. That was a high point for me—spending a whole day with one of my early heroes. The next year, we couldn't afford to bring anyone in as guest speaker, and they asked me to do the honors. Well, it certainly was an honor, and I think I did pretty well, but I was one of the youngest and least experienced ministers in the whole area. Somewhere in the mix, I was asked to speak on a religious radio program, although I don't now remember how many times I did that. The point is that I was asked to teach and preach in settings that don't usually come along when you are so young and inexperienced. God must have enjoyed watching me sweat it out and pretty much bluff my way through.

Theresa and me during the Preston Road School of Preaching days

Then there were the years of teaching at Preston Road. Being there opened all sorts of other doors of opportunity. I was Eldred's fair-haired boy as a graduate and representative of the school, and he took me under his wing. He often took me with him in his plane on recruiting trips, since I was an example of what he was trying to get prospective students to do. We golfed together, traveled together and became close friends in spite of our significant difference in age. I suspect many of my opportunities came from his recommendations, but the opportunities indeed came. I spoke at multiple congregations in the Dallas area for different events, from simply filling in for a local preacher on vacation, to gospel meetings to lectureships. Even though I was in my thirties, enough came my way that I started losing the too-young-too-soon feelings. My fellow faculty members, all my seniors in age and experience, treated me as a peer. We had close relationships and did things together outside the school setting. It was a small school anyway, with only about sixty full-time students (all men) and four faculty members plus Eldred as the director.

Since the school was based in Dallas, a city full of Churches of Christ, we had many visiting speakers in town that Eldred invited to speak in chapel. I thus rubbed shoulders with many of the more recognized preachers that I had previously only known by reputation. In those chapel services, I heard some great speakers and great lessons. I also heard just a few not-so-great speakers whose nervousness caused them to say some humorous things (to their great embarrassment, I'm sure). Once Eldred invited a new minister to the area to be our speaker in chapel. He was a middle-aged guy who brought his wife and one of his elders with him. His subject was about the nature of the church, and his point was that the church was not just an organization; it was a living organism. Since that was his sermon theme, he mentioned it over and over in the lesson. His problem was that from the very start, he used a word that involves bedroom activity in place of "organism." He must have repeated that phrase at least a dozen times: "The church is not an organization; it's an orgasm." As you can see, although the teaching program was very intense, the tension was lessened through different sorts of comic relief.

By this point in time, campaigns of the type I described earlier had morphed into less-intense types of public outreach, but evangelism was still emphasized. Somewhere along the line, "soul-winning workshops" came into vogue. The largest was the Tulsa International Soul Winning Workshop, and thousands flocked to Tulsa to hear classes of all types, but especially to hear highly motivational speakers at the night services who had reputations for leading churches that were converting many people every year. Although I was never one of these main speakers there, since I wasn't leading a church, I was still viewed as the Preston Road guru of evangelism, and so I was invited to speak at these kinds of workshops all over the country. Pretty heady experiences for a still-young guy.

Most of the schools of preaching were quite far on the conservative side doctrinally. Many of the teachers wouldn't have been too comfortable with some of the soul-winning workshops, since they viewed a number of the speakers as being too "liberal."

However, since I taught in one of the more conservative schools, I was asked to speak at very conservative events as well. The most conservative (legalistic) preaching school was in Tennessee, and in one calendar year I spoke on their lectureship program (my lesson being in a book with all other lessons delivered there) and in the Tulsa workshop. When I shared that with my preacher friends back then, they were a bit shocked. Because of both my interests and training, I traveled in both circles, and they were generally very different. By now, although still quite young, I didn't feel too young and that I was doing things too soon. I had become a part of the establishment, probably part of more than one establishment, oddly.

The Northwest provided a number of opportunities to hone my speaking skills.

The wild adventure stage continued in my life, but for some years it was to a lesser degree. I had to go through another stage of life and ministry before the adventuresome part returned in force. That stage was what I call in the next chapter a growing disenchantment. Actually the disenchantment started in some ways fairly early on, but I was young and resilient, plus the adventures were so new and exciting that they kept the negative feelings in the background (most of the time). You will see what I mean as we continue. Keep reading.

Chapter Nine

A Growing Disenchantment

Ministry Education in the Mainline Church

Unexpectedly, my disenchantment with the mainline churches began with my opportunity to pursue more education. When I accepted the teaching position at Preston Road, I knew that I needed to get an advanced degree in biblical studies as soon as possible. Therefore, I started planning for that as soon as I agreed to move back to Dallas as a teacher. Since I had once tried to figure out a way to attend Harding Graduate School of Religion in Memphis (Harding School of Theology), I thought choosing this school was a logical choice. I planned to move to Dallas in May 1974 and then continue on to Memphis to start school there for four classes that would take up the whole summer. We found an apartment close to the school and the congregation we had decided to attend, and we made the move. Right away I ran across a fellow student who was a golfer, and since there was a public course directly across the road from the campus, we played together one Friday morning before I went to the school office to settle the final details about my coursework.

I was very excited about attending that summer, having grown to love the academic life while a student at Preston Road, in spite of the rigors of that program. At Preston Road, the curriculum consisted of thirty-two Bible and Bible-related courses, each including fifty-four hours of classroom teaching. Add to that research papers, copious amounts of materials to be read, literally hundreds of verses to be memorized in a semester's time, and difficult exams to be taken; it was indeed a rigorous program. But I loved it all. Thus, when I arrived in Memphis that first summer, I was anxious to dig more deeply into the Bible and be inspired to be and do more for Christ. I had been accepted into the program and awarded a half scholarship, which was especially appreciated since our funds were at low ebb. Given my great anticipation, what happened next was very hard to understand and even harder to accept. I had walked into an atmosphere of which I was totally unaware and got blindsided as a result.

That atmosphere needs some explanation, for it was complex. Let me begin by saying that it was 1974 when I first started attending Harding Grad School. That was forty-two years ago, and I'm sure that what I am going to describe has since changed in myriad ways. The staff is totally different and the very atmosphere of higher learning in mainline churches has changed. My experiences back then would not occur now, and although they were more negative than positive, for reasons I will note, they have nothing to do with the present day in that institution. I have recommended the program to a number of my younger friends who are pursuing graduate degrees. I am not trying to cast any aspersions on that school or any other. I'm just telling my history, a history in this case that is four decades old. Much changes in forty years; I've certainly changed during those decades, mostly for the good, I pray.

The kids had to adjust to apartment living while I attended Harding Grad school.

The background of academic education in Churches of Christ was hardly on the radar during the early days of the Restoration Movement. Formal educational opportunities were scarce for most of those who wanted to preach. Self-education was the order of the day, plus being mentored by older preachers. In time, just as secular colleges were springing up in many places, those in the Churches of Christ were establishing Christian colleges for the general education of young people in this movement of churches. Ministry training was an important part of their early focus. Much progress was made in this direction, and the young men who wanted to be ministers attended these schools if they could afford it. Those who couldn't continued to be trained in the old way: self-education and mentoring by others. In the meantime, the various denominations had made much greater strides not only in offering undergraduate training, but also in training at the graduate level for ministers. By comparison, Church of Christ ministers had less formal training than did most of those in other religious groups. Some, however, went to schools not affiliated with Churches of Christ for graduate training, and as this number grew, their desire to see their movement pursue advanced degrees grew accordingly. Among those now thus academically inclined, just underneath the surface was insecurity about how our ministers compared to those in other groups regarding academic training. A lack of more modern approaches of training ministers was looked upon as outdated and inferior. For some of these academic types, the ministry-training situation in Churches of Christ as a whole was a bit of an embarrassment. This atmosphere added to the pressure of some wanting us to "measure up" to other denominations.

At the same time, many other leaders were not nearly as interested in formal, academically recognized training programs, but still saw the need for training more ministers. In the early 1960s, Sunset School of Preaching was begun, and it was followed by the establishment of many similar schools, including Preston Road School of Preaching. These preaching schools were designed to take students of any age, educational background or experience and train them in a packed two-year practical program to become preachers. In time, more and more churches wanted their ministers to have a more recognized academic type of training and the schools of preaching started dying out. One point is important here, namely that these schools like Preston Road weren't offering inferior education, far from it in my experience, although they were not accredited schools. For example, two of the teachers I had at my alma mater later joined the undergraduate Bible faculty at Harding University in Searcy, Arkansas. Sunset still exists in the form of the Sunset

International Bible Institute. Few others remain. The atmosphere and attitudes about ministry training are now much like those found in any popular denomination.

Since I mentioned Christian colleges among Churches of Christ, I will add some further background regarding them and their driving purpose, especially in the early days. Most parents didn't want their children to attend state colleges and universities for fear of spiritual contamination. Of course, we are all familiar with the challenges of Christians in state schools and know that the dangers are real. But since some students attended state schools anyway, another program was developed to help protect them, called bible chairs. Bible chairs became quite popular, and likely still exist in some places, although not as many as in the 1960s and 70s. Churches would procure a facility near the colleges, preferably across the street from the campus, and hire a minister with the academic credentials to offer Bible courses for undergraduate credit. But the main reason for the origin of bible chairs was to offer a place for Church of Christ kids to find fellowship with those of like mind and not be overly influenced by those who had different beliefs than they, or worse, no beliefs at all. In the case of both Christian colleges and bible chairs, the goal always seemed to me to align more with the Old Testament than the New Testament. The goal wasn't evangelism but to remain separate from the world. In the late '60s, another campus approach was begun in Gainesville, Florida that was designed specifically to be evangelistic. That movement, eventually called the Crossroads Movement, was successful in reaching the lost on the University of Florida campus, but it was viewed by most of the leaders outside Gainesville as liberal, dangerous and a probable cult. More about this subject later, but this background is a part of Restoration history and I thought it should be included here.

But back to my story at Harding Grad School. Some of the teachers there were very sensitive toward nonaccredited ministry training. Its affiliate, Harding University in Searcy, Arkansas had a Bible department and was training ministers at the undergraduate level, but they decided to hop on the bandwagon of the Preaching School Movement and start their own similar program. They called it by a more impressive name, but it was patterned after the preaching schools. One of my brothers-in-law attended Sunset and another attended the new school in Searcy. According to the reports I heard, some of the faculty members at the grad school were livid about what the university had done. That was about the time I arrived in Memphis. The deck was stacked against me from the start, for I was one of those preaching-school-trained guys. Thankfully, most of the staff wasn't so wound up about the whole scenario, and they treated me well. Unfortunately, there were a couple of notable exceptions.

I'll give you one example, just to show you how people with my background were viewed by the champions of academia. On that Friday morning I mentioned, after my golf game, I went to the school office to meet with the appropriate dean. We chatted nicely for a while, arranged my classes for the summer, then all of a sudden he exclaimed, "What are you going to do about those twenty-four semester hours of Bible as a prerequisite for entering the graduate program?" I didn't know what he was talking about. I had already been accepted and granted a half scholarship. I replied that I had more hours than that from Preston Road, to which he replied, "That doesn't count, because it isn't an accredited program." I was in shock, just having moved my family and rented an apartment.

I started trying to share what the program I had completed was like and how it was likely much more demanding than an undergraduate Bible course in a Christian college. That clearly got under his skin and our conversation went from bad to worse. I said some things I shouldn't have, as did he. In frustration, I suggested that if Bible knowledge was the concern as an entrance requirement, why not give everyone enrolling an in-depth exam, and the ones who passed it would be admitted and the ones who didn't, wouldn't. I knew what I knew, and I dare say not many enrollees could have matched my grade on such an exam. You can imagine how that comment was received! (Well, probably you can't.) By the end of our meeting, he had set up my schedule to take two summers worth of graduate courses, plus others by examination, all of which would count as undergraduate credit. I couldn't believe what happened. I had walked into something I didn't then understand (and still don't condone in any way).

I didn't personally know the dean of the graduate school, Harold Hazelip, but I knew he preached for the congregation that we had planned to attend for the summer. He was just getting back from a mission trip and must have been jet-lagged and very tired. But I was desperate. I waited in the parking lot of that church on Sunday morning until he arrived, and I told him of the bind I was in. I'm sure that was the last thing he wanted to hear when he had just returned from his trip, but he listened to my plight and said we would talk further. I started attending the graduate class Monday that the other dean had arranged, which according to him was going to count as undergraduate credit. After class was over, I went to Hazelip's office and we continued our conversation from the morning before. He spent some time trying to find a way to get me into the graduate program, and after about twenty-four hours, figured out a legitimate way to do it. I won't give the details, but Harold was, in my mind, one of the really good guys. I ended up having to go to him over the heads of others twice, and he came down on my side both times. I was highly appreciative of what he had done for me, but those who were on the other side, both of them people in high places in the school, weren't appreciative at all (to put it very mildly).

Harold Hazelip

I'll just leave it at that. In my anger and bruised pride (not justifiable, mind you), I just determined that I would make all A's in their school. Some of the students who attended during the regular school year warned me against taking certain classes in those short, three-week summer sessions, but I had no choice. I've never attended any school as demanding as Preston Road, and that included two graduate schools, so I was never worried about making the grades. I took the supposedly hard courses, played golf twice a week and still made my A's. However, the whole experience was an early stage of my disillusionment with the mainline church. Preaching school training was definitely very academically demanding, but very practical and very evangelistically focused. For the most part, I found graduate school training to be neither of the latter two. But I was pretty sure that the future was going to go in their direction, and that has proved true. However, advanced academic training has not stopped the consistently declining membership number of the mainline churches. As I said earlier, I trust that many changes have occurred in the past four decades in these types of graduate schools. I have no problem with ministry guys from our present movement attending that graduate school and similar ones, under certain conditions. Graduate school isn't for everyone, but I have been supportive of the right types of our leaders attending—and will continue to be. However, their zeal for evangelism cannot be lost in the process.

Evangelism on the Wane

Another factor in my growing disenchantment was the wane in evangelistic focus. The soul-winning workshops and similar events were starting to diminish. Those that remained were becoming more about meeting the needs of the saved than reaching the lost. Churches were becoming more inwardly focused and pulling back money from missions to spend on new buildings or new additions. Bigger and nicer church buildings were being built, many with basketball courts for the youth in the church. I saw it happen in churches of which I was a part and in churches I was quite familiar with. When I started training in 1970, and doing some preaching as I trained, evangelism was much more of a focus.

I recall reading an article by Gerald Paden in about 1990 after I was in Boston. He was one of the teachers at the Sunset School of Preaching, which had always had a strong emphasis on mission work. He and his brothers had all been missionaries at one time, as I remember it. Anyway, he wrote that the high-water mark of mission work by Churches of Christ outside the United States was in 1975, with 800 mission units (a unit defined as a couple or a single person) serving in mission points. He said that by the end of that year (1990), the number would have dropped below 200. I couldn't find the article now, but I've repeated the details so many times that I'm pretty sure the numbers are fairly accurate. Thus, when I speak of the wane in evangelism being disillusioning, it was not in my imagination, and what Gerald wrote coincided almost exactly with what I had observed. Within the past few years, I talked to a minister in a well-respected congregation in Tennessee, who himself is definitely evangelistic. He said, "Gordon, you would be impressed with what our congregation does for the poor, but when I mention evangelism, the standard response is 'That's just so 70s.'" Sad back in my days with the mainline church and sad now.

My sense early on that the churches in this movement were in a state of decline proved to be quite accurate. When I wrote the second edition of *Prepared to Answer*, in a chapter entitled "Restoration Churches," I included this observation:

> One fact seems sure: at the beginning of this century, the mainline Church of Christ is in the midst of an identity crisis. This crisis appears to be founded on two basic issues: loss of membership and a growing rift between the more progressive congregations and the more traditional ones. In the most current issue (February 2009) of a popular mainline Church of Christ publication, the *Christian Chronicle*, both of these issues are chronicled. (Note that I often use the term mainline Church of Christ simply to distinguish it from our own movement, popularly called the International Church of Christ.) Under the heading on the front page, "Church in America Marked by Decline," an official study identified 12,629 noninstrumental churches with 1,578,281 members. Those figures are said to represent 526 fewer churches and 78,436 fewer members than six years earlier.[5]

My recent research of the mainline church has shown that the decline continues. Later in this book, I will describe what was called an open forum at the Abilene Christian University Lectureship program in 2004, in which we had panels from both our movement and the mainline group sharing. To the chagrin of some, the oldest mainline panel member, Jim Woodruff, said several times that their churches were in the last days of a dying movement. He obviously was well acquainted with their trends and statistics. In the last chapter of this book, I am going to take an honest look at where our movement is, based on our own trends and statistics. The similarities are not going to be highly encouraging, but I have been on this merry-go-round before and I know what it looks like and where it leads, and I'm convinced that we simply have to face some realities if we are to stop our own cycles.

A Life-Saving Decision

I taught at Preston Road full time for just four years, although it had been my dream job at one point. What I was seeing disturbed me. When we graduated a new class twice a year, the graduates went out with a "Let's win the world" attitude. When they found out how few in their churches shared that attitude or could be motivated to share it, they did one of two things: Some fairly quickly gave up and quit preaching. The rest just adapted to the status quo and lost their zeal. Both of these reactions made me question why I was doing what I was doing. Eventually, I decided to leave the school. Usually, preachers found new jobs before quitting the one they had. I resigned without any prospect of a job, just to make the point that I thought the system was broken. I can't say that all of my attitudes and motivations were totally spiritual, but I was disenchanted enough to resign. We were somewhere in the middle of a semester when I informed them, because I wanted to give them time to find a replacement for me. The students were disappointed with my decision, and telling Eldred was hardest of all—about like telling J.T. when I left Vancouver. Both men loved me and had poured a lot into me. But I felt I had to do it.

Then once I had made my point of resigning without another job in view, I had to start looking for one. A large church in Oklahoma contacted me and asked me to come up for a weekend to speak and interview, so I took my family and did that. It was a wealthy church, with large, fancy hanging chandeliers in the auditorium. They wined and dined us (without the wine) and seemed very positive about having us pursue the job further. Then shortly thereafter, an elder from a church in the Northwest spoke in chapel at the school, mentioning that they were looking for a pulpit preacher, having just hired a campus minister from Texas. His presence struck me as a bit odd, since I couldn't recall an elder ever speaking in chapel. It was always a preacher. I spoke to him after chapel and mentioned I had been in the Northwest before and might be interested in returning. We set up dinner for that evening, and he was very encouraging about me coming up to interview. That was a surreal trip. We stayed with this elder, and he was one of these "Holy-Spirit-led" types, making me a bit uncomfortable back in those days.

He had set up a meeting with one of the women in the church who was a realtor, just so we could figure out the lay of the land and the price of real estate. We saw a house that we really liked, and he advised us to put in an offer on it, contingent on us getting the job there and selling our house. We did it, but our heads were spinning. Then we returned to the elder's house and had just been given a glass of tea when the phone rang. His wife went to answer it. We had just put our house on the market that Saturday, and this elder said, "That will be your realtor on the phone saying that they have an offer on your house." He was exactly correct, and since the offer was a good one, I accepted it. What a strange Saturday that was! But things were going to get stranger. I preached the next morning and evening, and then we had dinner with the elders. They informed us that if they hadn't already set up an interview with another person for the next weekend, they would have been ready to make a decision. Well, the meaning of that statement was completely obvious. When we caught the plane that evening, all of the elders and their wives wanted to see us off at the airport, which they did. We left flying high, in two ways.

Another surreal moment occurred the following Sunday, when I was preaching at one of the larger churches in the Dallas area. A group was taking us to the local country club for lunch (nice perks in those days with larger churches). As I walked out the door after preaching to get in my car and head to the country club, I had a shocking thought come from nowhere: "They are going to hire the other guy in Seattle." I wasn't even thinking about it, and had never even considered it as a possibility. I was pretty confident in myself about that time, given all of my experiences and success. But that's exactly what happened, as I found out later that evening. It put me in a depressed state for a month.

I then called my contact in the Oklahoma church (I think it was in Tulsa) and turned down the job there. He was shocked and quickly said, "But we've got it narrowed down to three guys and you have the most points!" I asked what in the world he meant by the most points. He said that they judged the applicants on everything with a long list of what they were wanting in a preacher. He shared that they had started with forty-two applicants and it was down to three with me on top of the list. I thought to myself, "Isn't that amazing, coming in first out of forty-two in one place and last out of two in the other!" Such is life, but I just didn't feel right about the Tulsa job and I wasn't sure why. It didn't take too many months to figure it out. By the way, I talked to a leader from that church in Seattle some years later and found out that the one they picked over me only lasted about six months. He apparently had some doctrinal issues to go along with some poor judgment. His last sermon was during a Sunday evening service, and I was told that he announced the title of the sermon as he began: "How to Have Spiritual Intercourse with Christ and Achieve Orgasm." It served those leaders right! (just kidding).

As the heading to this section indicates, a life-saving decision fits into the mix somewhere. I took another job in the Dallas area, as the preacher for the Buckingham Road Church of Christ. I stayed for three years, and it was a

At Buckingham Road, Tillet S. Teddlie with nephew, a hymn-writer of some note in the church (center).

good three years. I left the school in June and started full time with Buckingham Road at the same time. We found a nice house in the area and settled in to our new role. Interestingly, shortly after moving back to Dallas at the end of 2014, this congregation had a fifty-year reunion weekend celebration and asked us to attend and for me to deliver a lesson. It brought back a lot of good memories, and I appreciated the opportunity very much. But back to the past—1978 was the year I left the school. In February 1979, Eldred and three other staff members from Preston Road had flown in his plane to Abilene for the Abilene Christian College Lectureship. On the way home late that evening, Eldred tried to execute an instrument landing in a dense fog and crashed the plane. All four men were killed instantly. One of those men was on the faculty because I had left.

Eldred Stevens, with my two kids about to fly in his airplane. Eldred would later be killed in an airplane crash. I was lucky not to be on that trip with him.

Since the school had filled two slots, I don't know which of the men died in my place, but one of them did. I visited their widows, knowing that they knew what I knew in that regard. I was glad to be alive, but it took me a long time to get over the realities of that situation. The elders at Preston Road called me early the next morning and asked me to come spend the day with the students, helping them deal with the shocking, and shockingly sad, reality. I had been a popular teacher there and most of them knew me. It was a long day. They had lost their faculty, and I had lost two very close friends and one stranger who died in my place. The elders asked me to start teaching part time, along with some other part-timers from the area, until they could rebuild the faculty. My elders at Buckingham Road were quite willing, and I continued teaching on that basis until we left Dallas in 1981 to go back to the Northwest (not Seattle).

The Straw That Broke the Camel's Back

We moved to Tacoma, Washington in June, where I assumed the role of pulpit minister. We had a few others on staff, but I was the new designated preacher man. Just prior to moving there, some unusual events occurred (so what's new, huh?). I had preached one of the main nighttime sermons at the Northwest Soul-Winning Workshop in 1979, and Chuck Lucas, who led the controversial Crossroads church in Florida, heard the lesson. On the basis of that one lesson, as far as I know, he advised Tom Brown, the campus minister in Boulder, Colorado, to try and get me hired as the pulpit minister there. I had heard about all of the controversy surrounding their movement. When Tom started trying to get me to move there, I wasn't interested. It wasn't because of the controversy—I was rather intrigued by that—but because the elders in Tacoma had been working on me for a couple of years trying to get me to come there. Tom persisted, and I finally sent a couple of cassette tapes of several sermons to their pulpit-search committee in Boulder. One of their elders was very offended by the strongest lesson I sent, and he singlehandedly ruled me out and said to take me off the list. That didn't bother me at all, since I had already decided to go to Tacoma.

However, Tom must have felt bad about it, because he invited me to speak at the Rocky Mountain Evangelism Seminar in Colorado. I think it was, in his mind, sort of a consolation prize. That is how I met the Campus Ministry Movement (my term for it at that stage). That seminar changed my life. A few months later, just prior to moving to Tacoma, I made a one-week trip to Gainesville just to check things out for myself. I stayed with Joe and Sandy Woods, since I knew Joe, who was

Tom and Kelly Brown were leading the campus ministry in Boulder, Colorado.

in charge of their ministry training. He and I had been in graduate school together and he was a beloved friend. (He remained that for the rest of his life, until it was suddenly cut short some years back. He was a dear, dear friend, a Nathaniel if ever there was one.) Chuck asked me to speak there on a Sunday night and then invited me back that August to speak at the Florida Evangelism Seminar, quite a large event. I had just moved to Tacoma in June, and due to the controversy about Crossroads, one of my elders said that if they hadn't already agreed to me speaking on that program, they would have asked me not to do it. I replied that those types of decisions weren't going to be made by anyone but me. I would rather have been fired after two months than after I had bought a house and gotten settled in more. That same elder ended up being the straw that broke this camel's back.

    We stayed in Tacoma four years, during which time I tried to introduce small-group Bible talks and discipleship partners. Some of the younger ones bought in, but few of the older ones. I was patient and kept trying to get this mainline group to become more like what I was seeing in the Discipling Movement. Alas, to no avail. The elders had agreed to get with me for a discipling time once a week on an individual basis. Only one of the three had his heart in it; the others only knew I might leave if they didn't agree to it. Finally, this one elder said some things in our early morning time that showed me they were not going to back any real changes in the church, as I will describe a bit more fully in Chapter 14. I went home extremely discouraged and disillusioned. I wanted to tell Theresa I was going to resign and join the Discipling Movement, but I had moved her and our family around so much by then that I was afraid that she would be upset and totally resistant to the idea. So, for a change, I decided to approach the subject slowly and softly. I simply asked her how she was feeling about the church and its future. She was totally on board with all that I came back with from my preaching jaunts to discipling churches. We had two couples from Crossroads in our congregation, and she spent much of her time with one of the sisters, evangelizing and studying the Bible with women. At any rate, another one of those shocking surprises occurred that morning. Uncharacteristically for Theresa, she said with a very forceful and frustrated voice, "These leaders are not going to let us do the right thing. We are wasting our time here and might as well get out of here!" After I picked myself up off the floor, shocked to the core at what she had said and how she had said it, we started talking about our options. That was some mystery morning, and marked the beginning of the end of our mainline journey. Part Three will pick up from right here with an even greater mystery morning the very next day. Read on...

---

5. *Prepared to Answer, Second Edition,* Gordon Ferguson, Illumination Publishers, Spring, Texas, 2009, p. 116. Available at www.ipibooks.com.

PART THREE:
**THE DISCIPLING MOVEMENT
AND MY WILDEST ADVENTURE YET**

Chapter Ten

A Phone Call from an Angel

The morning after that frustrating then shocking morning, I headed to the church office in my three-piece suit and tie, as usual. Back then, we dressed up on a daily basis and kept regular office hours. I'm not sure why, but it was the order of the day. I had just gotten settled in my office with my head still spinning from the day before. Theresa and I had made the decision to join in with the Discipling Movement of churches, but we had no idea how to go about doing that. In the middle of that dazed and confused state, the church secretary buzzed me and informed me that some man from California was on the line. I picked up the phone and it was George Havins, one of the two elders from the discipling church in San Diego on the other end of the line. He got to the point quickly. In brief form, he said that they were sending their evangelist, one converted and trained at Crossroads, to Boston for further training. I knew enough about the situation to know that this particular evangelist had difficulties in relationships with older authority figures, including the elders. I had made one trip there before, not only to do some preaching, the public reason given for me being there, but also privately to meet with the evangelist and the elders. I enjoyed the speaking part of the trip, but the private peacemaking attempts appeared to be unsuccessful, made certain now by the phone call from George. The verbiage regarding further training was a convenient way to say that their evangelist was relieved of his duties.

George went on in our conversation to say that he and Ron Brumley, the other elder, wanted me to consider becoming their evangelist. After having served almost four years by then in Tacoma, only to have decided to leave the day before, receiving this invitation the next morning was more than surreal. As I was talking George, I was looking out of the window in my office toward and silently talking to God. What a shock that call was, and what a welcome shock! To me, that was a phone call from an angel, an angel named George. Of course, he wasn't officially offering me the role, but we set up a trip for me to speak, meet people and in a practical way, go through an interview process. But it was clear from the start that the job was mine if I wanted it. As I recall, this was sometime during the fall of 1984, so we set up a prospective trip to California during the Christmas holidays. This time, I didn't talk to my local elders about my plans until the details of the new job were definite. When I did tell the Tacoma elders that I was leaving, it was near the beginning of the new year and was accompanied with the request to stay as their pulpit minister until the end of the school year. That turned out to be a mistake, as such arrangements are apt to be, but I will leave out the details of that part. It wasn't just that I was in some senses a lame duck; some leaders and their wives took my resignation in a very personal way and interpreted any mention of my new job as an unfavorable comparison, in spite of my good intentions to just help them make some improvements in their congregation.

Ron Brumley, George Havins and Gordon Ferguson, leaders in the San Diego Church

A Willing/Unwilling Associate

During the four years we spent in Tacoma, I made many trips to speak for discipling churches. I kept crossing paths with Gregg Marutzky, then a young campus minister in Boulder, where he was being trained by Tom Brown. Gregg expressed a desire to work with me, which was flattering for sure, although at the time we were a part of two different movements. That's only partially true, actually, in the sense that the Boulder Church of Christ was mostly a mainline church, with a strong campus ministry led by Tom, who was converted and trained at Crossroads. I was talking regularly on the phone with Gregg, and I told him about our decision and the call from San Diego. At the same time, the pulpit minister in Boulder was leaving, and Gregg wanted me to consider moving there instead of California. By then, Tom had started a new church in Berkeley, California and had left Gregg in place as the new campus minister in Boulder. Gregg was from Colorado, loved Colorado and had just purchased a new house. While he definitely wanted to work with me, he definitely didn't want to leave the mountains.

Of course, that same elder who ruled out any consideration of me as the pulpit preacher some years back was still there. Gregg assured me that he was now open to considering me. Mostly as a concession to Gregg, I agreed to make a trip there prior to the one to California. The only thing that went well on that trip was the dinner with the elders before the meeting with them. I really enjoyed eating in a very nice restaurant. The aforementioned elder and I locked horns within five minutes of the start of our meeting. Gregg's face during the rest of the meeting is a bit hard to describe. He was definitely not a happy camper. But the meeting went as I expected, and I was on the plane the next day headed home, anticipating our trip to California even more. The atmosphere was a bit tense between me and Gregg, which I understood, given his disappointment after that meeting with the elders.

We made our trip to California a few weeks later, and it went as well as the other trip had gone badly. Ron and George, the two elders, told me that they knew I would want to disciple them and were fine with that. I didn't say anything at the time, but I knew it would be a two-way process from the beginning (and wanted it to be). They were older than I and had experiences in a discipling ministry that I hadn't had. I have never served with two finer elders than these. They became my very close friends from the start. George has been dead for some years, but those years serving with him in San Diego were amazing. I've only worked with two elders in my life that had a certain unique blend of qualities, George and later a fellow elder in Phoenix, Jerry Jones. Both of these men had very soft hearts and could shed tears easily, but when hard stands had to be taken, they never hesitated for a moment. It is a blend that very few have. Most tend to either be sentimental, making it difficult to take hard stands when needed, or they don't have enough empathy, and that hurts them and others when taking the hard stands. Ron was likewise a great elder (still is), with a great (and crazy) sense of humor combined with great wisdom. Their wives were ideal in their role as elders' wives. After my former experiences, I thought I had died and gone to heaven!

Gregg Marutzky and family came from Boulder and joined the staff in San Diego.

Once we accepted the work, we began making occasional trips to San Diego to teach and look for housing. I also kept in contact with Gregg, who had mixed emotions about moving to California. He loved his ministry in Boulder and, I'm sure, felt an obligation to Tom who had trained him and left him in charge of the campus ministry there. When we moved to San Diego in June, we had only a very small group of staff members left there, most of whom were young and inexperienced interns. The older ones had gone to Boston with the former lead evangelist. It was obvious that I needed help on staff, and Gregg in my mind was where we had to start. What happened next may appear at first glance to be a bit questionable, perhaps involving a type of blackmail, but in context it was needed and the description is accurate. I think you will also find it humorous.

The San Diego church had been financially helping out with the Berkeley planting. Because of that, Tom made occasional trips to speak in San Diego anyway, and I urged the elders to have him back sooner than later. After he spoke for a Sunday service, Ron, George and I took him out for lunch at a nice restaurant. Although we took our time painting the big picture for him, the bottom line went something like this: "Tom, we have been happy to help out your work in Berkeley and want to continue doing so. However, our ability to do that depends on our congregation continuing to do well, and right now we have serious needs for additional staff. We need to have Gregg move here, join the staff and help us plan the future. Therefore, we need you to persuade Gregg to move here." Tom had no problem understanding the point we were making, and he evidently didn't have too much of a problem making the decision to do what we asked. Gregg and Cathy moved shortly thereafter, and we began inviting others to join our staff based on his recommendations. He had connections that I did not, and without his help, I shudder to think what might have happened. Most of those we brought in did very well, and some, like Mike and Libby Rock, have remained very close friends until this day. Moving from a new home in his native Colorado was not easy for Gregg, and we had a few bumps to work out in the early days, but God blessed the move even on a personal basis. He and Cathy converted a couple in their apartment complex who became very influential leaders, a couple that I still see from time to time when I am visiting California.

Beyond All Expectations

When we arrived in San Diego, we were excited but definitely apprehensive. I had never led a discipling church, and I found myself leading meetings the likes of which I had never even attended—Bible talk leader meetings and house church leader meetings being among them. Gregg and I teamed up for much of it, which certainly helped, and the elders helped as well. At the first house church leader meeting I led, I started out with a biblical lesson of some type, but then kept asking the group what they normally did next. Ron and George hung around until the fellowship time ended and everyone else had left. Then they sat me down for a little chat. They said that leaders had to instill confidence in whatever group they were addressing, and to be asking the group what should be done next was hardly the way to accomplish that goal. They instructed me to ask them in advance if I was unsure about how to lead a given type of meeting, but then to take charge and lead it—confidently. Good advice. From that point, I did what they said, and proved an old adage to be true: "Fake it 'till you make it!" That approach is not hypocritical, by the way. It is doing what is best for the people you are leading. It worked wonderfully.

Due to the legalism of the former leader, the church was on the legalistic side. But the positive result was that everyone did everything that they were asked to do. I told Theresa that I might not know how to build such an atmosphere from scratch, but I was going to do everything I could not to mess up what was there. I never did tell the group that I thought they were legalistic; I just started teaching Romans at all-church midweek services. When you added the element of grace to the existing element of exacting obedience and participation, it was like throwing a match on gasoline. It was beautiful to behold. The year prior, the church had baptized 115 people, their best year ever. Due to the transition time of almost half a year, the baptism count for the present year was fairly low. However, things began to explode evangelistically. In one Bible talk leader meeting during the early fall of that year, I asked how many baptisms they thought we could have by the end of the year. Different numbers were thrown out and finally one brother yelled "160!" I thanked him for his faith, but said why don't we shoot for 140? He obviously had more faith than I. We ended the year with 165. Just as encouraging was the fact that few left the church. The commitment level demanded and the fairly intense level of activity was never burdensome. People were as busy as could be in the church, but they were happy. It was much like that time in my hometown church years earlier when serving felt like a blessing and not a burden.

It was also an entrepreneurial stage in our movement. We didn't have everything systematized, but that was to take place later in Boston and be passed on from there. As a result, we dared to dream big dreams. We sent out mission groups to "spy out the land" in two US cities and in two foreign countries. We held three-day fasts, followed by a congregational devotional and all-night prayer meetings by house church groups. Gregg came up with the idea to have a two-week campaign during the summers, during which we would ask everyone to take their vacation time and move into the dorms at San Diego State University. Amazingly, almost every member did it! We knocked doors, shared our faith in every mall or other convenient place in the city, and did a lot of street preaching in public places. We also had a multitude of visitors attend our three Sunday services during that time and baptized many. It was heaven on earth to me (and to most others). We called it the *LIFE Campaign* (Love Is For Everyone). I've never experienced anything like that two and a half years we served in San Diego. As I recall, we baptized about 220 the second year we were there (the first full calendar year) and well over 300 the following year (just before we moved away). I could fill an entire book with the various stories of what happened during that amazing time. I've never seen it duplicated again anywhere I've been.

On June 19, 1985, just a couple of weeks after arriving, it was painfully obvious to me that I was in way over my head. While staying with George and Cleo for the first three weeks prior to moving into our own house, I went on a long prayer walk. I climbed to the top of a high hill in Poway, where they lived (and where the congregation had its beginning), and just looked over the valley and prayed. I told God that I knew we were going to lose considerable ground that year, given everything about the transition, but begged him to let us climb back up to where things were then by the same date the following year. On that exact date the next year, George and I were with one of those mission "spy teams" in Guadalajara, Mexico, eating and rejoicing in a huge restaurant serenaded by a loud mariachi band, having experienced a year that was so far beyond my expectations that I could hardly believe it. Those experiences were the norm, not the exception. It was a marvelous period of time for the church and for our family. I performed a number of weddings for staff and other members, and life was packed with living the Jesus life. Our two children were teens at the time, and the teen ministry, led by Charlie and Kathy Monticalvo, was likewise amazing. Thus, our first foray into the Discipling Movement in an up-close-and-personal way was truly a "God thing," for which we will ever be grateful. Some who weren't there might have a different view of what went on, but others besides me who were there have much the same memories as I describe here. Praise God!

Chapter Eleven

A Blizzard and the State of Shock

All good things must come to an end, as the old saying goes, and our time in San Diego was one of those good things (best things, actually). During the several years prior, it became popular for leaders to go to other places that were more advanced and receive more practical training. We had a number of leaders come to San Diego for that purpose, but most of the moving of this type was to Boston, which had become the leading church in our young but fast-developing movement of churches. Whereas we had been mainly a part of the Campus Ministry Movement for some years, we were becoming more and more a movement of churches. In the early days when the Crossroads church in Gainesville was the most influential church, they focused on training campus ministers to be sent out to existing mainline Churches of Christ in order to start evangelistic campus ministries in those places. This approach reflected a noble goal, but it was destined to fail, sadly enough. In my books *Prepared to Answer, Second Edition* (Chapter 6) and *Dynamic Leadership* (Chapter 11), I describe the reasons behind this failure. I would suggest reading both of these chapters in order to gain insight into this period of our history as we moved from being in the Campus Ministry Movement to becoming a church movement.

A Fateful Decision

The leaders in Boston began appealing to both Gregg and me to move to Boston for more training. By this time, the reason for the moves of receiving more training was augmented and eventually virtually replaced by the goal of uniting the movement. Whereas most congregations were still pretty autonomous, like the mainline groups out of which they came, it was becoming obvious that if the world was to be evangelized, we would need to be much more united and tied together organizationally. Although I think we moved from being independent to being too dependent from an organizational viewpoint, the idea was generally a right one. It took a significant crisis of movement upheaval to strike a more healthy interdependence, but in spite of some of the extremes reached, the unity did produce some amazing results in the area of planting new churches all over the world.

Sometime in the summer of 1987, Gregg and I, along with our two elders, Ron and George, made a trip to Boston to meet with their key leaders about this possible move to Boston. We met for several days, and there were definite periods of tension. Gregg and I were not excited about leaving San Diego, and our elders were far less excited (to put it mildly). We went back and forth in our discussions until I finally attempted to bring it to a close and agreed to move. Somewhat reluctantly, the four of us all accepted this decision and left Boston late one Saturday night to return to San Diego. Prior to leaving, everyone agreed to have Bruce Williams take my place in San Diego. It was a long flight after a very difficult decision, one that would be second-guessed for some time by the four of us, along with many others. None of our wives were even a part of the decision, something I would never repeat again. With little sleep, I had to preach the next morning in San Diego, after having told my wife we would be moving. Gregg and Cathy moved later that summer in order to start leading the MIT campus ministry that fall, and Theresa and I followed at the end of December. The months without the Marutzkys went quite well, showing that we had done a decent job of training those who rose up in their leadership level that fall. I was proud of them.

I told this story to a friend in the Dallas church soon after we moved here at the end of 2014, and he asked me a very direct question: "Was it the right decision?" In spite of having missed San Diego (both church and city) terribly, it was the right decision. It was hard on the family in some ways, the children especially, but so many blessings would have never come our way without the move. Almost immediately after arrival, Wyndham and Jeanie Shaw dug into our marriage in a unique way that changed us forever. It is not a matter of chance that they wrote the foreword to my book *Fairy Tales Do Come True*. In fact, had we not moved to Boston, I would never have become the writer and author that

I did. I have Randy McKean to thank for that, and I have thanked him publicly and privately. For many reasons, the move was the right decision.

A Rough Entry into Bean Town

I have never loved a city as I did San Diego. I must have loved it too much, in fact, so God ended our grand time there. Life as a disciple of Christ wasn't designed to be easy, except for brief respites, and that of my family was about to enter a tough phase. On December 30, 1987, we landed in Boston in the middle of a blizzard. I described it in my marriage book as "a blizzard so strong that the pilot of our plane circled the city until we were low enough on fuel that he had no choice but to land. It was our scariest landing to date (not nearly the only scary one of hundreds or thousands), and just prior to it, Theresa was singing softly the words of an old hymn: 'Dear Lord and Father of mankind, forgive our foolish ways…' And she wasn't kidding." The city of Boston was anything but love at first sight. We had moved from a four-bedroom, three-bathroom house at the foot of a mountain to a two-bedroom duplex with snow covering everything. Compared to San Diego, Boston looked old, dingy and dirty. However, I had convinced myself that it was God's will that we move there, and I was determined to make the best of it, and we did.

The church in San Diego had gone from a Sunday attendance of about 550 when we arrived to about 1250 when we left two and a half years later. So I went from leading this size group to leading a house church with about thirty-five members. While such adjustments were not easy or quick, believing it all to be God's plan made it tolerable. If someone had told me that we would live there sixteen years and grow to love the area as we did, I would not possibly have believed it. We had marriage problems that led to a radically changed marriage, and our children had a harder time adjusting than Theresa and I did. Our daughter, Renee, ended up attending four different high schools, which was not a positive experience for her. Our son, Bryan, had stayed in San Diego for several weeks after we moved in order to finish his first semester in college. When he landed in Boston, he had his surfboard with him and was wearing shorts and a T-shirt. That wasn't the best way to walk out of the terminal into another blizzard. But in time we all adjusted and started to feel the hand of God in it all. However, when Bryan had the opportunity to join the team planting the church in Honolulu just over a year later, he and his surfboard left Boston happily. Renee had to wait a few more years, until she graduated high school.

Anticipating a Quick Exit

Since by design we had been lured to Boston for more training, we anticipated a reasonably quick exit. I had always seemed to be able to learn and adapt fast, and fairly soon after moving to Boston, we were targeted to lead the church planting in Dallas. I already knew the language well and couldn't have imagined a better fit for us. We began making trips to Dallas, since a small group with interest in joining the movement was already here. Our new fairy tale was beginning to take shape.

For Nick to take Gordon's place, Gordon's books had to fit Nick—and they did!

On one of those trips to Dallas, a bootmaker from San Antonio presented me with a special pair of cowboy boots that were made for a member of the Dallas Cowboys football team, my longstanding favorite team back then. This player had paid a substantial down payment for these quite fancy, unique boots but had never claimed them. Since I have a narrow foot, I couldn't imagine the boots actually fitting me, but I very much appreciated the gracious gesture. To my amazement, the boots fit perfectly. Obviously, this was a sign from above that we were destined to end up in Dallas!

Because of our age and counseling experience, we often worked with the two elder couples in Boston at the time, the Gempels and the Bairds. That was special for us, and it never occurred to us that our relationship with them was going to destroy our Dallas planting dream. They suggested to Kip McKean, then lead evangelist, that I be appointed as an elder. I remember him approaching me at a wedding and raising the possibility. I immediately replied that I had absolutely no interest in being an elder. I was destined to be the evangelist planting the church in Dallas (where I had lived three times prior, by the way). He said that I could be appointed as an elder and then, after serving for a year, lead the planting to Dallas. Something in my gut didn't like the feel of that, but I ended up agreeing and was appointed as an elder in May 1989. Just prior to the big Boston Evangelism Seminar in 1990, after I had already made plans for a recruiting meal for the Dallas planting during the seminar, I received a call from Kip, asking me to come over to his house. With a pit in my stomach, Theresa and I drove the few miles to that house to meet with the McKeans, the Gempels and the Bairds. They informed us, in a nutshell, that I was more valuable as an elder in Boston than as an evangelist in Dallas. The death of my dream led me into a grief process that lasted about a year.

After remaining in Boston for sixteen years, having supposedly moved there for more training, one of my San Diego friends said to me that I must have been a really slow learner! One thing I never have learned to do well is to say no, that's for sure. One thing I have learned to do pretty well is to trust that ultimately, God is always in control, even of the little things, and in time he will work it all out for good. That was certainly the case in Boston. Nick and Debbie Young moved to Boston into a ministry group that we were overseeing by then, and we discipled them until they led the team to Dallas. We went with them in order to help out in counting the cost with the members of the little group that was awaiting our arrival, many of whom are still here twenty-five years later, as are some of the original members of the team from Boston. Our initial arrival in Boston in the middle of a blizzard was a shock to the system, one of many such shocks we would experience before we left. Our sixteen years there were a combination of the good, bad and ugly, as I will discuss in the next chapter. But my tendency is to forget much of the negative in time and remember the positive. Since we left in December 2003, I have often prayed to God and said to others that those years were as a fairy tale to me, and such they were.

Chapter Twelve

The Good, the Bad and the Ugly

Please keep in mind as you read this chapter that in spite of the bad and the ugly, to me the good outweighed them. That observation reminds me of the lesson that I preach over and over and over. Life on this earth is not designed to be heaven. If we expect it to be, we understand neither God nor the Bible. Since it is not designed to be heaven, we can expect our share of challenges. They are intended to help mold us into the image of Christ, and we are molded more by our reactions than by our actions. We choose both our actions and our reactions. We also choose how we are going to view the negatives that occur in our lives. They can be stumbling blocks or they can be stepping stones. I truly believe that the challenges I faced in Boston were stepping stones. Whether or not I counted them all as joy as they occurred (James 1:2), I did understand that they produced a harvest of righteousness and peace as I was trained by them (Hebrews 12:11). I feel sad for those who also faced the good, bad and ugly in Boston and allowed it to produce bitterness in them. I understand the temptation to allow hard times to affect us in that way, but I also understand that it is not biblical and therefore not acceptable to God. If you fall into that category regarding your suffering of any type, please reconsider.

As I describe my experiences in Boston in these three categories, rest assured that I don't describe them because of ill feelings toward anyone. I am going to be honest about what I think happened and why, because I think it important for others to understand better how the history of the Boston church unfolded. My perspective is my perspective, as I have already said, and you don't have to agree with it. But I do ask you to consider it. If we don't learn from history, we are destined to repeat it. Some parts of my history I would love to repeat; other parts I would be loath to repeat. However, it is all part of what made me who I am, and

Bob and Pat Gempel, Theresa and Gordon Ferguson, Gloria and Al Bairf, elders and their wives. At one point, they were the only elder couples in the ICOC family of churches.

I like to think I learned much about how to handle success and failure, positives and negatives. Hopefully, my experiences will help you discover practical lessons that will aid you in becoming a better you. That is God's goal for all of us.

The Good–Relationships and Opportunities

Being in Boston allowed Theresa and me to develop some of the most special relationships we have. Some of God's finest have been a part of the Boston church and many remain there. I could write a long, long list of people with whom we shared special relationships and built a massive treasure house of memories. Life is about relationships, and thus the Bible is of necessity about relationships, starting with God and then with his children. I mentioned those early days getting help from Wyndham and Jeanie Shaw. In time, Wyndham and I served as elders together and made a great team. Theresa and I also became a team with Tom and Sheila Jones, first in a discipling relationship and then in a partnership with Discipleship Publications International (DPI). We had countless experiences with these two couples that will forever be etched in our hearts and minds, some that made us cry, some that made us shriek with laughter, and all of it deepened our spirituality.

When I became an elder, we joined the Gempels and the Bairds in that role. We spent much time together due to our shared role, and Theresa and I learned much from each of those four. At one point, when the elders in San Diego had resigned, we three elders in Boston were the only three in our movement. Thankfully, that scenario has changed much through the years and needs to change much more by adding additional elders all over the world. As might be suspected when dealing with some of the very serious situations with which we had to deal, we had our disagreements and tensions. I think those caused us to grow closer to God and closer to each other. I treasure those years together.

After Randy and Kay McKean came in as lead evangelist and women's ministry leader, we had a learning curve in figuring out how to work together as a new team. The Gempels left Boston first, followed by the Bairds later, making it vital to appoint Wyndham as an elder at a relatively young age. Dan Bathon became the lead administrator for all of our New England churches as well as those in continental Europe. He and his wife, Julie, were already good friends with the McKeans, coming to Boston with them from the Paris church. Randy chose his key evangelists to join the rest of us as a leadership group in Boston, but the idea of a true leadership team wasn't yet a pervasive idea in our movement, and we had to forge how we were going to work together. We had some grinding of the gears in the process. The group varied at different times, as some couples moved in and others moved out, but I have many good memories of times together with everyone who was a part of the various leadership groups at any given time.

Some relationships were more natural for me than were others, as is always the case with human beings. Randy wasn't as easy for me as some others were, and I'm quite sure I wasn't as easy for him as some others were in his life. But we had a good working relationship and I learned a lot from him. In spite of some of the occasional tensions between us, he gave me some of the finest ministry opportunities I ever had. Once the Gempels

*Wyndham and Jeanie Shaw, Theresa and Gordon Ferguson (back row)
Kay and Randy McKean, key leaders in the Boston Church of Christ*

and Bairds left Boston, Theresa and I were the first in the main leadership group to have an empty nest. As a result, Randy started sending Theresa and me to help out with young churches in Europe. Boston through the years planted over fifty churches (which planted yet others), and the McKeans dearly loved Europe (still do). In 1991, Theresa and I started visiting churches in Europe, some older ones but especially younger plantings. At that time, we were having a Euro Conference every summer, and Randy's creativity made for some truly outstanding programs of this type. Theresa and I made at least one trip annually to Europe and often two or three. Typically in the summer, we would visit two or three churches for several days each, and then end up in Paris for the Euro Conference.

We sometimes made unscheduled trips to deal with ministry emergencies. On most of these trips, Randy and perhaps others would go also, but they left more quickly, leaving us behind to follow up and make sure the problems were resolved. Randy and Kay had children still at home, plus they had their leadership roles in Boston as their top priority. I remember one such trip when I packed in twenty minutes and Theresa and I left for five weeks, dealing with one of the more serious situations we ever dealt with in Europe. That was a gut-wrenching experience from a human perspective, but from a divine perspective, it helped save a church with very few casualties. We grew to love Europe and even all of the exhausting travel associated with it. I don't think we failed to visit any of the major cities in both Western and Eastern Europe. Randy touted us as the mom and dad of Europe, and that is how we were viewed and treated.

In the summer of 1999 at the Euro Conference, Randy and Kay asked to meet with us. They presented the idea of us moving to Paris for three months to help build family in our largest European church. Because of other obligations, we didn't feel that we could go as quickly as they had in mind (that fall), but we did go at the end of that year. Just at the end of the planned three-month stay, they decided to bring back to the United States the couple that had been leading the Paris church for some years, so at the last minute we were asked to stay and lead the church until a permanent replacement could be found. We traveled all over Europe from there, and the six months living in Paris was one of the highlights of our ministry lives.

Another area of opportunity was in teaching and writing. In 1995, the then world sector leaders asked us to oversee the development of a children's curriculum, called the Kingdom Kids Curriculum. We assembled a steering committee of about a dozen people who were educational experts, plus brought in others as needed, and our times together were both lots of fun and very productive. The project became far bigger than anyone anticipated in the beginning, and at one point, we had over twenty people working for DPI just on the curriculum. When I reached the extent of my ability to pull it all together while trying to fulfill several other roles at the same time, Sheila Jones saved me by taking over my role. She brought it to completion in a great way, making me forever indebted to her.

DPI had been started several years earlier, with Tom Jones being the editor-in-chief. Tom and Sheila were on the ministry staff when we first arrived in Boston, but Tom's worsening multiple sclerosis forced them to resign their roles. Tom worked in the church office for some time, until Randy McKean and Dan Bathon approached him about heading up a publishing program, which ended up as DPI. At about the same time, Randy approached me about ceasing to lead ministry groups as an evangelist to become a teacher (while also remaining an elder). I began writing study-guide booklets and conducting teaching days for the whole church about twice a year. Randy named those days "Bible Jubilees." In 1995 I wrote my first two books, *Prepared to Answer* and *The Victory of Surrender*. Second editions of both are still available and have been widely read in our movement. They have also been translated into other languages. The opportunities to write and conduct Bible jubilees were exceedingly special ones for me, as were the trips to Europe for Theresa and me.

Tom and Sheila Jones

Randy also asked me to start teaching the ministry staff of New England, and soon thereafter, the European staff. We had three-day teaching sessions, complete with advance reading and followed by a final exam. Randy and Kay took every course and every exam and had all leaders at any level do the same. When I started a full-time teaching ministry at the age of sixty-five, I conducted similar training programs in Asia and Kiev, and the leaders there participated at the same level Randy and Kay had. Not all leaders follow that example, an irritant to me, because I've never met any leader (including yours truly) who couldn't use additional training or refresher training. Actually, Randy and Kay already knew more Bible than most leaders I have worked with anywhere and both are authors. I just wish all leaders were as anxious to keep learning and to set an example of participation in the same way that they did.

Many other relationships and opportunities during our Boston years could be mentioned. I hesitated to mention the ones I did, because there are many more very special relationships and opportunities that came my way in Boston. I do want to end this section by telling about one early and one late relationship that developed, each of a unique type and very special. Dave and Peggy Malutinok moved to Boston right after we did, and we discipled them for a number of years. Not long after they moved in, Peggy gave birth to their second son. When another brother and I went to visit them in their hospital room, Dave held his newborn son up and asked me, "Would you like to hold Scott Gordon?" That was some unexpected surprise, and the Malutinoks have remained very special friends since that early beginning. The latter unique relationship was with Valdur and Irene Koha. We knew them through the years in Boston, but not very well. God worked it out for us to become very special friends after we moved from Boston. I'm not sure how he accomplished that unusual feat, but he did, and I am most thankful. I could write an entire book on our Boston years, but I must move on to the more negative aspects of the Boston experience. Of course, when I say negative, we should understand that God works in mysterious way, and what often seems negative to us is used positively by him. Only he knows his plans, so once again, what you have here are my perspectives of my experiences.

The Bad and the Ugly

When we arrived in Boston, I was struck with the differences between there and San Diego. The San Diego church may have been in the entrepreneurial stage, but the Boston church was already systemized and growing more in that direction. Numbers and statistics were far too important in my opinion, but I was there to learn and I went along with the status quo while fighting to maintain good attitudes. Of course, some leaders of influence filtered what was passed down, and I was fortunate in my earliest Boston days to have Wyndham in charge of the ministry of which I was a part. He and I wrote a book entitled *Golden Rule Leadership* over a decade later, but he was always a Golden Rule type of leader. In the book, our intent was to simply show that golden

Gordon Ferguson and Wyndham Shaw and the release of Golden Rule Leadership

rule leadership included team leadership and treating those whom you led as you would want you or your own children to be led, in age appropriate ways. That wasn't the case with some other leaders to whom I had to answer. But since I moved up the levels of leadership fairly fast, I was spared a lot. God protected me. At the same time, I did things in leadership in trying to fit into the system of which I am now ashamed and for which I have apologized many times. The real problem for me in Boston was that so much good was being done that it was difficult to sort out the difference between what was good, what was bad, and what was good intrinsically, yet applied badly. It was at times, a tricky path both to understand and to negotiate.

The Kip McKean Chapter

When I arrived in Boston, Kip was the lead evangelist and met with me twice a month for discipling times. He always treated me fairly, and I didn't have some of the personal conflict with him that some did—at least until much later. From what I understand, during his earliest days in Boston, he was less rigid and demanding, and those in the church had more flexibility in how they did ministry, even under his leadership. If true, he became worse and worse, ultimately resorting to a truly military style of leadership that very unfortunately trickled down to how the average member was treated. You can read more about that in my book, *Dynamic Leadership*, Chapter 4. Kip's father was an admiral in the Navy, the equivalent of a general in the Army. Kip is a military thinker and thus needs an army and an enemy. With him, there are two types: those who are with him one hundred percent and those who are against him.

As the movement grew and more and more churches were planted, Kip decided to assume the role of missions evangelist for the whole movement and to appoint world sector leaders as those directly under his authority to carry out his directives. I never had a problem with the organizational aspects of this structure; it was the military implementation of it that was wrong. When Kip resigned as lead evangelist in Boston, he gave this role to Tom Brown for a year before Tom led the planting to Los Angeles. Once Kip started traveling around the world to assist other churches, his rigidity increased. For one example, he kept saying to us when he was in Boston that we were the "faith center" for the rest of the movement and thus had to set the growth curve for the movement. With the New York City fast-growing church down the road, situated in a city with over four times the population of Boston, such expectations for Boston were not just unrealistic, they were absurd.

The focus on number of conversions increased more and more in intensity. This was also the period when church "reconstructions" were in vogue, and the same practice started being applied in Boston with their larger ministry groups (called zones at the time). The reexamination of one's baptism had an integral connection with the reconstruction approach, and many of those already baptized were rebaptized (most of them didn't need to be, although some did, for various reasons). In staff meetings when baptisms for the week were announced as part of "taking stats," many of them were rebaptisms. I recall Tom Brown saying that we had to focus on having more "Gentile baptisms," meaning those not already involved in the church. Once Kip removed the "Jewish baptisms" from the stat reporting, their numbers abruptly dried up, which says a lot about the unhealthiness of the numbers focus and the pressures accompanying it.

During that time, we began having weekly new-Christian orientations, conducted by the lead evangelist and elders. Although all types of people need to be converted, converting those with weaker characters without converting enough people with leadership potential is a poor path to take, and the long term results are easy to predict. Those orientations to welcome new Christians made it obvious that we were following a poor path.

Finally, Tom taught a lesson in a staff meeting about being the light, the leaven and the salt. He commented that we had to reach more true Bostonians, and not just the foreign-taxi-driver types. I thought it to be one of the finest and most needed lessons I ever heard in a staff meeting, and after that Theresa made pumpkin bread and we began meeting our neighbors in our nice neighborhood. We were so excited and determined to do the types of things Tom had suggested. But alas, Kip came back to town from a trip shortly thereafter and saw that the baptism numbers were down, and we returned to our old ways of short-term building approaches (which eventually imploded). That gives you an idea of the sort of pressure cooker we were all living in. Ministry had for me moved almost totally out of the blessing category into the burden category.

Gordon and Theresa at a Middle East Conference

One last illustration to show how bad things got under the watchful eye of Kip: The church held another Bring Your Neighbor Day, with the usual goal of having a one-to-one ratio of visitors to members. Kip was on another mission trip when the Sunday event occurred, but he came back to town shortly after. We had many visitors, a number that we would salivate over today, but we didn't hit our stated goal. Kip preached for staff meeting, and did he ever preach! At one point, he hit the little music stand that he used for a podium so hard that his notes went flying. That blow was accompanied by the loud and angry assertion that "this was a defeat worse than Pearl Harbor!" Wow—*Twilight Zone* material, at least in my mind. Such extremes were not infrequent, and further demonstrate why I say that Kip has a military mindset about nearly everything related to ministry. Increased pressure through focus on numbers and harsh accountability had to end up in a bad place, and we did arrive there.

The Henry Kriete Chapter

In February 2003, Henry Kriete, then an evangelist in London, lit the fuse that started a firestorm. I and a number of other leaders received an email from him containing a document entitled "Honest to God." Kip had been taken out of his leadership role in our movement for other reasons prior to this, but many more changes had to be made. Henry sent his letter initially to key leaders only, and I quickly wrote to encourage him and prepare him for the resistance he was going to face. While I didn't agree with everything he wrote, I did agree with much of it, and I knew that these issues would raise serious discussions that were needed. I assumed that he was trying to force the discussion among the key leaders, which is where it should have taken place, based on passages like Acts 15. In Acts 15, at the Jerusalem Conference, the membership was well aware of what was going on but trusted the leaders to meet privately and come up with solutions. However, I soon found out that my assumption was mistaken and Henry intended from the start to make his documents available to everyone. I have an email someone forwarded to me from Henry, showing that this was his exact original intent.

The problem with handling the situation like this is that it sent many people into what could only be described as a mob mentality. Open forums and written forums provided opportunities for a large number of people to vent their frustrations in ungodly ways. I have often stated that we had enough entrenched approaches among us that it was going to take a bomb to dislodge them. However, that bomb needed to be a "smart bomb" capable of dealing with the issues without creating huge amounts of collateral damage. Henry's bomb was definitely not that type of needed bomb. What ensued shook our movement to the roots and did some types of damage from which we have never recovered. The efforts I and others made to persuade Henry to write a second letter, encouraging the continued discussions but to conduct them in a spiritual way, fell on deaf ears, sadly. He was far more influenced by the voices of the mob than by voices of reason. Of course the letter also forced some much-needed changes, but that did not justify the unnecessary collateral damage of many people's faith. Some may differ from my assessment of the whole situation, but if so, I have to believe that I have many facts at my disposal of which they are completely unaware.

Major Results of the Upheaval

As soon as it became obvious how much of an upheaval was occurring, I knew at once what some of the very scary consequences were going to be. One, discipling was going to cease immediately for most disciples, and sins of all types were going to enter our movement as a consequence. They entered as predicted, since discipling, or "one-another" Christianity, is the greatest deterrent against it. Two, evangelism was going to come to a virtual standstill, since what we feel forced to do will cease when the agents of force are no longer active. Further, as church leaderships made needed apologies for the characteristic sins in our movement, one apology was that we had been too judgmental toward other Christian-oriented groups. The apology was good, but the lack of definition given left many of our members feeling that almost anyone who called themselves a Christian must be one, biblical doctrines notwithstanding.

Three, with people so upset at leaders, financial giving was going to take a very serious hit, which it did. As a result, many staff members lost their jobs and many mission points lost their support. We had planted many baby churches all over the world, and we essentially left them to die (and many did). The Kriete letter justly listed the sins of leaders, but most of what was listed applied primarily to older, experienced leaders, not younger staff members. Yet the incendiary nature of the letter left people with the feeling that all leaders were guilty of any of the sins committed by any leader anywhere at any time. Hence, we lost a generation of good young leaders. To me, it was an absolute bloodbath for which there is no excuse. I and many others like me had to be the ones to lay-off some really promising young leaders, and it was one of the most heartbreaking experiences of that whole era. Of course, going along with that concern was the loss of trust in leaders generally, no matter what kind of leaders they were. That was not only unfair, but the churches suffered as a result. Leaders were in a state of shock and many evangelists became clergymen (and many still are), changing the very character of our movement in many ways. I'll have more to say about that in chapter fourteen of the book.

Suffice it to say, our movement has never been the same, in both bad ways and good ways. I think God has used that time to help us make some needed changes. I think God also grieves over some of what has now settled in as part of our overall atmosphere and character as a movement. Along with most other leaders who remained on staff, I made many apologies publicly and privately. We did go along with far more of the negative practices than we should have, although as I said before, enough good was occurring to make it difficult to distinguish between what was actually bad in and of itself and what was bad only because of implementation (mostly having to do with wrong ways of motivating our members). It was a hurtful and confusing time for almost everyone. In time, reason and common sense returned to those who remained, and all of the positives were once again appreciated. For those who left, many of them have gone places that they would never have imagined, and the results have often been catastrophic in their personal lives. However, with God, all things are still possible and we all can, with his help, see more good days ahead. For that we must all continue in prayer.

Chapter Thirteen

From the Frying Pan into the Fire

During the middle of 2003, Theresa and I started considering moving closer to our grandchildren. Brad and Lori Bynum, dear friends, planted this seed in our mind originally at a lunch together. Brad kept quoting passages from the Old Testament about passing on our faith to our grandchildren. While we were initially resistant to the idea, within a few days we had started looking at the possibility with more accepting attitudes. We felt that Boston had adequate replacements for the roles we were carrying and that we could leave with good consciences. I'm sure that the events of my final years in Boston had taken an emotional toll on me, and that played into our decision. I contacted the leaders in Phoenix, where our daughter and her family lived, and a location far closer also to Hawaii, where our son and his family lived. The leaders there were very open to the idea and excited about it. The plan was for me to help them get an eldership established and continue my teaching role in some capacity. If such a move seemed to be jumping out of the frying pan, the reality was that we jumped right into a raging firestorm in Phoenix.

In Boston, friends and coworkers tend to make you feel irreplaceable, but no one is or should be. The idea wasn't warmly received by those closest to us. Many tears were shed and some tempers flared (very temporarily). I was sixty at the time, and it just seemed that the time was ripe for leaving. We had loved so much about our years in Boston, and that church will always be close to our hearts in a very unique way. Our years there defined who I was to be for the rest of my life, and I will always be thankful for the relationships and opportunities we were blessed with there. The elders asked us to consider staying for an additional year, which we refused. Then they asked us to stay an additional half year, which we ended up doing. We sold our house in the summer, moved into an extended-stay hotel and spent the remainder of the year trying to tie up all of the loose ends of our various ministry roles. The leaders in Phoenix were copasetic with the idea, and everything seemed grand. We had little warning of what was awaiting our arrival in Phoenix.

Into the Flames

The firestorm took longer to ignite in Phoenix than in other places. From the time we agreed to move there until the time we did in mid-December of 2003, the firestorm had spread unbelievably. Immediately after arriving, even with the moving issues themselves, Christmas approaching and family coming in to visit, we threw ourselves into the flames. We started with the most damaged region of the Phoenix church (out of five total) and started meeting every night and on the weekends with groups of six to eight people. Each of the groups was composed of those with strong opinions and attitudes, but varied widely in those opinions and attitudes with others in the group. There were about three different "camps" within the region, united for or against the various leaders in the region and/or the church. Prior to our meetings, those in the three camps had mainly talked over their views with other members of like mind. The old "birds of a feather flock together" principle was obviously in place. However, we chose these groups with which to meet randomly, resulting in many of those attending being absolutely shocked that others saw things differently than they did. It was very tense, but otherwise a good lesson on perspectives—how they are formed and how they are maintained. Basically, the different views are what held us together, at least for some time. Everyone was perplexed enough for a while not to feel confident in pushing their viewpoints too strongly.

In time, some left our church and some moved in, mainly from California churches. Our membership stayed fairly constant, just with different names and faces. Finances were an issue, for the contributions had dropped off significantly. We had to let go a number of staff members, which wasn't all bad. In my many years of ministry experience, I have never seen a staff that left me scratching my head as much as this one did. It didn't take long

First elders appointed in the Phoenix Valley Church

to figure out that some may have been adequate staff members at one point, but time and challenges had since rendered them unqualified. Others should never been on staff in the first place, and who put them on and why was a mystery to me. The problem was that replacing anyone we let go was a huge challenge in itself. More people wanted out of the ministry than to get into it, and given the firestorms, you really couldn't blame them. In the end, with the passing of a few years, almost all of the staff resigned or were terminated, and replaced with more qualified people.

The details of how it all went down were in most cases not pretty, but absolutely necessary. It took ten months to get an eldership appointed, and as the only one with a lot of experience as an elder, I had to be the trainer without being a "head" elder. That was some tightrope to walk. My constant message to the other elders was that the only consideration in making hard decisions was righteousness—determining what was the right thing to do. Thinking about possible reactions and repercussions could not be a consideration. That message was not an easy one to implement, but with advice from elders and other leaders outside Phoenix, we negotiated the firestorm and the difficult decisions, and that congregation is in a very good place today. We stayed there nine years, after our sixteen in Boston, and the details in both places could easily fill separate books.

Unique Opportunities

As is always the case, battles eventually end, and even in the midst of the battles, God sends blessings your way. We enjoyed our years in Phoenix and made many close friends and some enemies (more of the latter than anywhere before or since, actually). We did get to be around our two grandchildren in Phoenix and found it far easier to see those three in Hawaii as well. During our years there, I served as an elder for a number of those years, a teacher at times, and lead evangelist for a few years (unplanned, but necessitated by Joe and Annie Silipo, dear friends, moving to Los Angeles). All in all, given the number of challenges faced, it went as well as expected at the time and better than expected in the end.

A Surreal Trip to Abilene

Soon after moving to Phoenix, two events occurred that affected me deeply. One, my mother died about a month after our move there. She had been in a nursing home suffering with a rare disease, but losing our last parent was difficult, especially in the environment in which we found ourselves upon our arrival in Phoenix. Then another event occurred about the same time, and surreal is the most apt term to describe it. We had left the mainline Church of Christ almost twenty years prior and had little contact with anyone in that group since. I received a fair amount of opposition when I joined the Discipling Movement, and unfortunately dished some of it back in their direction. Gregg Marutzky was leading the Dallas church at the time and working toward a master's degree at Abilene Christian University, a mainline Church of Christ school. In talking with some of those in the Bible department, it was decided that a meeting between some key members of both of our movements might be in order. Enough time and change had occurred to suggest that some bridge building could be possible and well received. Gregg ended up asking me, Al Baird and Mike Taliaferro to join him on a panel to have an open discussion with an equal number of panelists from the mainline group (they had one extra). It took place at the annual ACU Lectureship in February 2004. They ordinarily had a several-day session called the open forum, designed to discuss controversial areas within their fellowship. Due to the nature of that year's discussion, they changed the meeting venue to a large one, anticipating a bigger-than-usual crowd in attendance. That turned out to be a wise choice.

One of the surreal parts of the experience for me was being back on a campus I had not been on for decades, attending a lectureship I had not attended for decades. Plus, I saw many people that I hadn't seen in decades, including many of my former classmates and students from the Preston Road School of Preaching. But the most surreal thing of all involved the date of my trip there. It was twenty-five years to the day since that plane crash in which I might easily have died on February 21, 1979. Eldred Stevens and Rudell White were close friends, and it was either Tom Dockery or Ray Evans who took my place in the plane. They flew to Abilene and back for the lectureship, and on February 21, 2004, exactly twenty-five years later, I flew to the same lectureship. I did wonder as I boarded the plane if destiny had me slated to die on that anniversary. Obviously it wasn't my time yet.

The time in Abilene turned out to be very enjoyable and reassuring. The crowds were large, and the panelists on from both groups worked well together. We met privately for times of planning, discussion and prayer. Our group was open about our mistakes and sins, and those attending seemed to appreciate what they heard. They were ready to forgive, bury the hatchet and let bygones be bygones. I received not a hint of any feeling to the contrary. The Preston Road school was still in existence at the time, under a different name and meeting in a different location in Dallas. I was invited to attend a luncheon they held for present and past students, and the friendly reception was refreshing. Since that time, over a decade ago, those from the two groups have intermingled much more, and although we differ on certain emphases, we are no longer enemies. Churches of Christ have almost from their inception as a restoration movement come in many flavors, so a continuance of this reality is hardly surprising.

Starting a Teaching Ministry at Age 65

About the time I was nearing my sixty-fifth birthday, the elders in Phoenix were discussing the budget for the following year (2008). It was becoming increasingly obvious that the church wasn't large enough to support me and Theresa in the role of teacher/elder and women's ministry leader. The discussion moved in the direction of needing to lay off our teen-ministry couple or our campus-ministry couple in order to keep us on staff. As an elder, I just couldn't approve doing that. So I told the other elders that I was going to have to help them fire me and that I would find another means to provide for us financially. Starting a teaching ministry seemed the best way to do that, and I had already had discussions with others about that possibility. Sometime during that period several had approached me about starting a training program in Asia, the one that ended up as the Asia-Pacific Leadership Training School (APLA). We had to figure out the financial details as well as design the whole program, but that was pretty much a bird in the hand. Near the same time, I had discussed with Valdur Koha the possibility of working with the European churches again. He was the chairman of both the Beam Fund and the European Mission Society fund in Boston. We figured out a way to make that work, so God was opening doors for me to start a formal teaching ministry, which began officially in mid-2008. I started traveling to those areas, and others as opportunities came along, and it was a very exciting (and exhausting) period of time for a sixty-five-year-old.

Gordon teaching in the Philippines

In 2009 at a church builder's workshop, I asked advice of a number of trusted brothers about what I should focus on in the future, in order to spend my remaining years in a way that would leave my best legacy after I was gone. The advice was unanimous: leadership training and writing. As much as I loved Europe, what

I was doing there didn't fit that definition. Therefore, I had a discussion with Valdur at the workshop and essentially resigned from the European work. That was a difficult decision for both of us because we loved working together, but he agreed it was the right one. I made one or two more trips to Europe that we had already planned, but after that, my only steady leadership training work was done in Asia, mainly in the Philippines.

God soon opened another door. Shawn Wooten was working with the European ministry staff, mostly those in Eastern Europe. We were together at a conference in Estonia and he asked me to teach his group one day, which I was happy to do. At the end of that one session, he said that I had to set up a leadership program in Kiev patterned after APLA. At that point, I didn't know Shawn well, but I agreed to pursue his suggestion. That led to many trips to Kiev and to developing a very close personal friendship with the Wootens. Theresa didn't travel often to Asia with me, but the Wootens wanted her to accompany me pretty often to Kiev, which she did. She and I loved Asia and the Ukraine and rejoiced at our many opportunities to travel to both. In both places, we had a part of the program designed

Gordon (with a translator) teaching in Kiev, Ukraine

for ministry training for the staff, but also a part designed to train nonstaff leaders (lay leaders as the religious world would term it). That part of the program grew amazingly, with more and more people joining. They came from surrounding countries and were excited to learn how to be better people-helpers. The memories of working with those two programs are some of my most special.

Houston, We Don't Have a Problem!

The writing part of my legacy focus meant figuring out ways

to write and promote my writing ministry. DPI was still operating at the time, and the Joneses graciously sold me all of their supply of my books. I purchased the rights to them from the Boston church, who held those rights from the time I wrote them while working in that church. Toney Mulhollan had started his publishing company, IPI (Illumination Publishers International), and he took over the marketing of my present and future books. He invited me to come to Houston, where IPI is based, and do a teaching weekend primarily for the singles ministry. He wanted to start making video materials available containing my teaching, in addition to my audio ones. Through his efforts, I've ended up with quite a list of both audio and video teaching series.

The heading of this section is based loosely on a movie line that you likely recognize. From that first trip, I developed quite a connection with the Houston church and its leaders. I made other teaching trips there and was invited to move there, which I couldn't do. However, I did tell one of the elders that I would be willing to come there as often as possible if they wanted to work out an arrangement for that. They called a board meeting and amazingly fast, they made me an offer that I couldn't refuse. They rented an apartment for us, and both Theresa and I made as many trips as possible for almost two years. We worked with the staff and other leaders in various ways, and for about six months I served as the congregational evangelist (at age sixty-eight, just about the time I found out I had a couple of heart conditions). It was an amazing time. One year I counted up the time I spent at home in Phoenix, and it was only about one-third. The rest of the time I was either in Asia, Kiev or Houston. I told someone that I was living with such a wild schedule because I was trying to outrun Father Time. We grew to love the Houston church in an amazing way, so much so that I dedicated the only book I wrote during that period of time, *Dynamic Leadership*, to them. It was a wonderful span of time, from 2008 to 2012. By the time I turned seventy, I had preached thousands of lessons of all types to all kinds of audiences, in hundreds of churches and other settings, and in scores of foreign countries and states within the United States. I had also written a dozen books and hundreds of articles and documents of all types. If I had died at the age of "threescore years and ten" (Psalm 90:10 KJV), I couldn't have wished for a more adventuresome life as a preacher man!

Two Short Stints in Two Different States Since (So Far!)

Near the end of our Phoenix years, Theresa was diagnosed with COPD (Chronic Obstructive Pulmonary Disease). She was sixty-eight at the time, and up until then had truly been the Energizer Bunny. The air quality is so poor in Phoenix that Theresa's disease, which included the development or worsening of both asthma and allergies, forced us to make the decision to move. At age sixty-five, retirement was out of the question for me, since I didn't find that concept in the Bible for disciples of Christ. So I told God in a prayer walk that any such decision to slow down would have to come from him, knowing that it would likely come through health issues for me or Theresa or both. Although I did develop some heart conditions while we still were in Phoenix, they were not serious enough to make me slow down, nor did the doctors ever suggest such. One of my ministry friends commented wryly that if the doctors had known what my schedule was, they might have had more to say about that. Perhaps so.

Some of the leaders in both Los Angeles and Dallas invited us to move to their locations and serve there. We opted for LA, where the air quality was good near the coast and terrible inland. Obviously we chose a place nearer the coast. That was an interesting two years. Their school of ministry had fallen into a state of inactivity, and they wanted me to help resurrect it. Although I had some issues with how that was done, I did the best I could and taught a number of ministry training courses during our two-year stint there. I also did a fair amount of preaching and teaching, with Theresa joining me in conducting marriage and parenting retreats. I love the leaders there, and all in all, had an enjoyable experience as we made many friends to go along with the old friends already there. It is hard to beat living in Orange County, especially the city of Irvine where our condo was located (on a golf course). I told Theresa it was like living in a time share for two years, and that's a pretty apt description.

Our son had been encouraging us to move close to them, for two reasons. One, he and his family wanted to take care of us as we aged and needed more help. Two, he and his wife, Joy, wanted us to be around his sons much more than we had in previous years, since they lived so far away in Hawaii. We had actually considered moving to Hawaii, at least for a year. But before our two-year commitment in California was up, they decided to move to the Dallas area to be near Joy's sister and her family, who had moved there. That led to us moving here at the end of 2014 after leaving Los Angeles, which worked out fine, since the Dallas leaders had already opened that door a couple of years prior. In 2015, I served on the ministry staff on a part-time basis, similar to what I had done in Los Angeles.

However, since my writing ministry was not really taking off, I decided to make 2016 a writing year, while I am still alive. It is difficult to write when you are dead, and I've already lived longer than I ever expected to. During this time I am not traveling out of Dallas for speaking engagements, although I am doing some limited speaking in Dallas. As I finish up the first draft of this book in a few days, that will make three books I have written in this year through May: *Fairy Tales Do Come True*, about our now-fifty-one-year marriage; *The Apostle Paul: Master Imitator of Christ*; and this present book. I am not going to ease up and retire after May ends, but I do need a rest. I will kick back for a little while, maybe even catch a fish or two. Three books in five months (four really, not having started in earnest until February) has been a bit much, and I want to proceed from here with a more sane schedule! Pray for me to do that, since long term workaholics aren't very good at stopping to smell the roses.

Chapter Fourteen

A Growing Disenchantment, Revisited

My initial title for this closing chapter was "Growing Old, Looking Back and Looking Ahead." That is pretty much what I want to cover in it. However, Toney had the idea of playing off the title of the last chapter in the mainline Church of Christ part of the book. I liked the idea and am thus using that title. However, my initial title is still true: I am growing old, I have spent the entire book looking back and I do want to look ahead. At seventy-three, most of my life is behind me, which gives me some unique perspectives that only age can bring. My experiences in three different but related types of churches has added to that perspective. I think I see things coming for my present movement because of what I saw in my past ones. I have some concerns that perhaps not too many others share, but in my opinion, I have good reasons for those concerns. You will have to make up your own mind about that as you continue reading. I am going to state my concerns in the form of questions, and you will have to decide if I am describing those concerns accurately and if so, how you are going to respond to them on a personal level. Ultimately, it is more about each of us and God than about our movement or another movement. I can't change a movement, nor can I change myself—but God, the relentless pursuer of souls, can.

What about Our Zeal Level?

When Theresa and I joined the Discipling Movement, the zeal level was almost miraculous to us, compared to what our previous religious experiences had been. The focus on total commitment was a constant reminder that to claim that Jesus is truly Lord means that the top priority in our lives is him and his ways. It means denying self, taking up a cross daily and following him—no matter where that leads. We all embraced the belief that disciples are willing to go anywhere, do anything and give up everything. We no doubt had a few fringe members, mostly in their hearts but not their actions. To be in a discipling church meant that everyone did everything asked of them. The zeal, commitment and activity level was quite something.

The Kriete letter and its immediate effects were highly alarming to me, as explained in a previous chapter. What I describe as the zeal and commitment level dropped off almost immediately for what seemed to be a majority. I kept preaching and teaching that danger lay ahead. Whatever level we settled into would become the new norm fairly rapidly, and changing it once it was entrenched would be all but impossible. As I observed the new norm being defined, I began preaching about my concerns but comforted myself (and others who shared my apprehensions) with the idea that at least we still had in our memory banks what it had been like and thus could be like again. The slowdowns were justified with rationalizations, such as that we had been too involved previously in church activities and had neglected our family in the process. So what did we do? Spent more time with our family doing things in the world around us rather than in God's world.

People began to pick and choose which church-related activities they would participate in and which they wouldn't. Leaders lost their prophet's edge and quit preaching strongly about what God's expectations were. In time, we became much like the religions around us. We had some members that continued to stay very involved and others who did their picking and choosing, and both were equally acceptable approaches in most churches by most leaders. Individual talks with those who were losing their commitment were no longer the norm. Perhaps from the pulpit the right standard was still being preached in many places, even most places, but what happened to the individual discipling that called people back to their own lordship commitment? For those of us who have been around for a long time, we know what it was like in earlier days and we know what it is like now and we know the difference, don't we? I have heard my little wife beg God in prayer many times to be able to live long enough to see us like we once were in our zeal level.

What about Our Discipling?

People have asked me many times through the years what brought me into this movement of churches initially. My answer has always been the same: discipling, one-another Christianity put into practice. My first sermon after meeting the Discipling Movement was entitled, "The Missing Ingredient." Those of you who have heard me preach about the subject or read my writing about it know what my convictions are. At age seventy-three, I need discipling. The idea that we need it until we reach a certain level of maturity, and not after that, is so ridiculous that I refuse to address it. Christ, with his character and actions, represents the biblical level of maturity the Bible calls us to. If you think you have reached that, you have ended up in exactly the same place where one of my mainline elders was in 1984. In what proved to be our last discipleship time together, he actually said to me that he already was enough like Christ and thus didn't need discipling. That one comment convinced me that my resignation was a certainty, for with leaders having such a warped view of the Christian life and of themselves, no real changes in the church would be possible.

Another similar idea that I have heard espoused among us is that we don't need discipleship partners (or a triad or some similar structured, regular arrangement), but when we hit a place in our life or family where we need such an arrangement, then by all means go and seek it out. To me, that idea (along with the previous one), falls under the heading of stupid drivel. Do you find that offensive? Fine—be offended (but keep reading). It all boils down to a lack of some type of effective organized discipling plan through which we can follow God's directions for putting "one another" principles between Christians into place. The lack of such a plan, in my firm opinion, explains the highly increased levels of marriage problems, family problems, divorces, addictions (especially pornography among the men) and assorted other potentially soul-damning sins.

Theresa and I were asked to speak at a retreat for elders and elders-in-training a couple of years back for congregations in a certain part of our country. One or more of the lessons was to be on some aspects of discipling. At one point, I asked representatives from each congregation represented to share with the group what was going on with discipling in their church. Very predictably, every last person said that they believed that everyone should be discipled and that the concept was biblical, but not a one of the churches represented had an organized program in which the large majority of their church was participating. I wasn't amazed and I wasn't shocked; but I was dismayed and saddened. It's the same story everywhere I've been for the past decade. At one point in our history, we boldly asserted that the Bible is not just full of nice ideals to sort of shoot for, but rather it is full of commands that God expects us to obey. We appear to have lost that conviction.

I met with a group of older leaders from the mainline church after moving back to Dallas, sometime last year. One asked specifically why I had left their group. I answered by describing my convictions about discipling. One of the men present, I suspect an elder and successful businessman, got a bit worked up and started preaching my sermon. He mentioned passages like James 5:16 and confession of sins to one another and said that they didn't come within light years of obeying passages like these (or something to this effect). He saw it clearly and quickly. He was so forceful in saying it that one of his friends gently censured him about his manner. I laughed and told him I understood, since my passions can cause me to say things pretty strongly and bluntly at times too. Right now is one of those times, if you haven't noticed it yet! I mentioned in a workshop fairly recently that I was old-school in that I practiced set discipleship times. An elder's wife came up to me privately and said that my statement sent shivers up her spine and weirded her out. Listen, I understand that many of our practices in the past, discipling being one of the foremost on the list, were implemented in hurtful and sinful ways. Plenty of practices, in and out of the church, have been implemented in bad ways. That does not invalidate the correct practice of those things. This business of dragging around the mistakes of the past on an individual or movement basis and letting them keep us from obeying God has got to stop, and it needs to stop *now*.

What about Our Personal Evangelism?

The Great Commission is still in Matthew 28, the last time I checked it. Sadly, this is another key area that we implemented badly in many ways and turned people off to as a result. There was a time when we were in studies with non-Christians regularly and shared our faith even more regularly. I hate the fact that we turned it into a numbers game and an obligation rather than an opportunity and a blessing. Satan surely loved those distortions. But it is not about obligation and being pushed; it is about having the heart of God and imitating Jesus. We can no longer hide behind the bad motivations of the past in this area or any other area as an excuse for disobedience. We equally need to get back to the good part of our past history and refuse to tolerate the bad part of it. I had a mainline Church of Christ friend once who visited the church in Boston decades ago. He asked some young married woman if she shared her faith regularly (perhaps it was daily). She looked at him quizzically and didn't understand the question. Finally, she figured out what to her was a weird question and said something to this effect: "Of course I do; I'm a disciple." When was the last time you were in on a sit-down study with someone? How often do you share your faith?

To be candid, this is the one area I pray about most in confessing my sins of omission. I am not consistent. I share my faith pretty regularly overall, but I go in spurts. Sometimes I share several times in a day and sometimes I go several days without sharing. I'm not being legalistic here and I'm not saying that we have to share with a new person every day. But I am saying that evangelism is a consistent part of the lifestyle of a disciple. It is a highly important part of imitating Jesus, who came to seek and to save the lost (Luke 19:10). It is also a highly important part of imitating Paul, who asked us to do so (since he imitated Christ). Listen to his heart in this passage:

> *And pray for us, too, that God may open a door for our message, so that we may proclaim the mystery of Christ, for which I am in chains. Pray that I may proclaim it clearly, as I should. Be wise in the way you act toward outsiders; make the most of every opportunity. Let your conversation*

*be always full of grace, seasoned with salt, so that you may
know how to answer everyone (Colossians 4:3-6).*

What about Our Group Evangelism?

I enter this part of the discussion with some trepidation. I don't want to discourage you. I don't want to scare you by using statistics, but statistics have their place. In the past, we used them as motivation rather than for aiding in evaluation. My doctor uses statistics—lots of them. I'm glad that he does. When a test result is bad, we look for solutions together and I come back to be evaluated even sooner than normal to make sure my health isn't going in a downward direction. We have to look at ourselves in the area of evangelism, but we also have to look at what is happening in our group, our church, our grouping of churches in a geographical area, and then overall as a movement.

After the Kriete debacle, we lost thousands of members overnight. Most of them didn't leave us seeking another church. Rather, they left God. Some in both categories have come back; most haven't. I'm very grateful for the ones who have, but our restoration numbers are in steady decline during the past five years. It took some years for our movement to return to the point of positive growth. Truthfully, we were struggling with growth before the letter, although still planting churches. I mentioned in an earlier chapter the open forum at the ACU Lectureship in 2004. The oldest panelist was with the mainline group—Jim Woodruff. He is a highly respected preacher and author, a man with a very kind personality. When he made the comment about their group that they were in the last days of a dying movement, some of his fellow panelists didn't like what he said, and they spoke up. That didn't deter Jim in the least, and I remember his saying it three different times, in both our private meetings and in the public one. Why wouldn't he back off? He knew their statistics and downward spiral in growth, to the point of decline in membership and numbers of congregations. Are we prepared to look at ourselves that honestly? I pray that we are. I appreciate many things about our movement. I also appreciate a number of things about my mainline church background. But my appreciation doesn't tempt me to be sentimental. The facts are the facts are the facts.

So what are the facts about our growth as a movement through the end of 2015? Let me share some with you.

- Overall growth for our movement of churches in 2015 was 1.9%.
- Overall Growth for the US/Canadian church was 1.3%.
- Our 20 churches with over 1000 members grew less than 1% combined.
- In those largest churches, it took 1175 members to produce a growth of one person.
- Of these 20 churches, San Diego had the most percentage growth (6.1%), while 8 of the 20 actually lost members.
- No churches in our movement grew by 100 or more.
- 70% of our total churches are under 100 members.
- We have 667 congregations overall, 381 of which baptized between 1 and 10 people, and 122 had zero baptisms. Thus, of our 667 churches, 503 (75%) baptized between 0 and 10 people in a year's time.
- My home state of Texas shows a 5.5% increase in membership in the last year, from 2939 to 3101, an increase of 162 members. But we had 328 baptisms and restorations. Due to our increasing number of children maturing, we have been blessed with many teen baptisms (my grandson being one of them), but how many in our communities are being converted is an important aspect to consider. Texas also benefitted by having many Christians relocate here over the last several years because of a robust economy which has skewed the actual net growth numbers.
- As of the end of 2015, we had just over 100,000 members worldwide. Compare that with the fact that the global human population growth amounts to at least 75 million annually (well over 200,000 every day).

Church growth doesn't tell us all we need to know about church health, but it obviously tells us something — something vitally important. What do these statistics mean? That our fastest-growing churches are growing slowly; that many churches are stagnant in growth; and that some are shrinking. Overall, we are hardly making a dent in a world population that is increasing every day at more than twice the size of our total membership. Unless we begin reemphasizing and reimplementing the "multiplication principle" (every member converting one person per year) that we taught with such vigor in the past, we will do little to alter these results. When I preached for mainline churches, we grew. The other leaders were in fact quite encouraged by our growth, especially compared to many other congregations. My consistent comment was that if all congregations grew at the same rate we were growing, the huge majority of the world's population would still die without ever having heard the true message of Christ. We had a fatal flaw in our thinking, in that we were comparing ourselves with ourselves. Here is what Paul said about that practice: *"We do not dare to classify or compare ourselves with some who commend themselves. When they measure themselves by themselves and compare themselves with themselves, they are not wise"* (2 Corinthians 10:12). My question to us is this: are we not starting to do the same thing to feel better about ourselves?

What about Our Unity as a Movement?

A good minister friend of mine once told me that as a brand-new Christian, a leader told him that the biggest challenge for our movement was destined to be unity. He hit the nail on the head. A lack of unity guarantees failure; the presence of unity guarantees success. We all know that in our past history, we were too dependent on each other in leadership structure, and local churches that were mature with their own leadership were often controlled too much by leaders outside their congregation. We have repented of that but swung the pendulum too far in the opposite direction. Now many churches are very independent and pretty closed to outside involvement, even when they obviously need help. Interdependence is the right balance, with a genuine openness to get help from the outside when things are not going well. And let me state the obvious here—when seventy-five percent of our congregations are baptizing between zero and ten people per year, things are not close to going well.

We are overly fearful of organizational structure that could help with our problems. In a nutshell, we are afraid of Big Brother (whoever that could possibly be now) coming back in to tell us what to do. Most of those with such fears, in my experience, have backgrounds in the mainline Church of Christ, who are known for, and take pride in, their autonomy. Having seen the fruits of that in two different movements, my mainline background moves me in opposite directions as I know their failures all too well. In our early days as a movement, we still had roots in that background and were clearly influenced by it in areas like the use of instrumental music in worship and in our views of the women's role, to name just two examples. We finally eradicated these traditions in our group, but it was neither quick nor easy. The more subtle elements that come from that background are harder to detect, but for many, they are still there and are hurting our unity as a movement. We already have a structure in place that is working to some degree and could work to a far greater degree. Our clearly identified geographical families of churches could be of tremendous help if we could embrace the right kind of interdependence and welcome an infusion of help from leaders within our own area. But for this to become a functional reality, we are going to have to discard our fears and restore a brand of unity that we do not now have, at least in some parts of this country and perhaps in other countries. If we don't, the concept of congregational autonomy is going to stop the progress that could be made. Cannot we learn that from the mainline churches?

How about Another's Long-Term Perspective

Toney Mulhollan is the editor of Illumination Publishers International (IPI), and has been since its inception in 2003. He is not only my publisher but has been a special friend and coworker for decades. Toney, who has a background in the Church of Christ, made a visit to the Crossroads church in Gainesville, Florida when still a teen. He saw so much excitement and felt so much electricity in the air that he promptly moved there at age nineteen. He served in the printing ministry there for eight years until moving to Boston in 1987. He moved to Boston to set up a printing ministry, which eventually became part of Discipleship Publications International, and lived there until 2006 when he moved IPI to Houston, Texas.

So why have I asked him to write his perspective to end this chapter? For several reasons: One, he has been with our movement through all of its various stages. He has traveled all over the country recording seminars and visiting churches. He has over 25,000 sermons in his personal library from leaders across our movement. Few others can claim his breadth of exposure. I cannot. Two, because of that, his perspective needs to be heard and his experiences have earned him the right to be heard. No one among us has published more of our books or listened to and produced more of our audio and video materials than he. Therefore, he knows us and what we teach in great detail. Third, in our many conversations through the years, via emails, phone calls and personal visits, we discovered long ago that our perspectives regarding where our movement has been, and now is, are extremely similar. In a word, we share many of the same concerns, especially now. Therefore, I thought he was the ideal one to have the last say in this chapter, and I pray that we are all listening with open ears and hearts. Help us see what we need to see, Toney!

Toney Mulhollan

Commitment Then and Now

Though only my personal view, here are some disturbing trends that serve to illustrate the differences in what our movement was like in the early days compared to the present. These do not reflect the total situation in every church, but to some degree impact every ministry in our movement.

I vividly remember my introduction to the beginnings of our movement in 1979 when I moved my young family from Texas to Gainesville, Florida. I had no job and moved sight unseen to a church because of their teaching and the impact they were making. They were preaching "total commitment" to Jesus, no matter what stage of life you were in—whether you were a campus student, single, married, married with children or a senior adult, that was the expectation you were called to. I was pleasantly surprised to find that with few exceptions this was reflected in the Crossroads church.

The young men who were being trained there and sent out to plant campus ministries in established churches found that was not the case in those churches. Preaching total commitment eventually proved to be the ultimate factor in unsettling these older churches. Older members felt challenged with the call to discipling, evangelism and in general, radical repentance and openness. It eventually became clear that the majority of the older church attenders were not going to accept this invasion into their settled and comfortable lifestyle (especially from young novices in the faith). They appreciated the baptisms, growth of the church and the general excitement of seeing lives changed, but felt that this was for the youngsters. Most members and even leaders (preachers and elders) became defenders of the status quo. I even remember one church conference where a panel discussed the implications of the "total-commitment" theology, and a preacher proudly and defiantly proclaimed, "We will not allow even one ounce of total-commitment teaching in our church." And he didn't.

Every year, *The Christian Chronicle* printed a list of the churches baptizing over 100 people. In 1980, at the height of the Crossroads Campus Ministry Movement, more than one-third of those churches had Crossroads-trained ministers. As discussed in this book as well as others, within a decade virtually all of these churches eliminated their association with the campus ministries. Looking back, I can say without exception that every one of these churches declined in growth, influence and commitment. Eventually, *The Christian Chronicle* no longer printed the yearly list of churches baptizing over 100 (for obvious reasons).

Now some thirty-five years later as our movement has aged, I'm hearing some of the same attitudes emerge. Recently, in a discussion with a minister of one of our churches, a brother talked about the need to call people back to "total commitment" to Jesus. The preacher said, "We can't call the people back to that kind of commitment; they won't stand for it." Upon hearing this, I thought to myself, "He's probably right." We have become our fathers. Some of the very things that disturbed us about the mainline churches and their lack of commitment we are now struggling with ourselves. Our growth has stagnated, our zeal level has diminished and our commitment to discipleship has become in practice something considered optional. And most disturbing, just like the mainline church, we now have defenders of the status quo.

Zeal Then and Now

My first visit to a Crossroads Church of Christ service was overwhelming. I had never seen anything like it. The second I walked through the double doors of the auditorium, I could feel an electricity in the air. There was a "buzz" about the fellowship. It was as though a reunion of a loving family was taking place that hadn't happened in years. People were talking, laughing and encouraging one another, and there were numerous Bibles open as people shared with each other truths being learned from God's word. There were even groups of people praying together. And that was all before the service began!

When the service started the energy only increased. It felt like every member was in the choir. My eyes scanned the auditorium and I couldn't find anyone that wasn't singing. There were no part singers with microphones up front, or loud musical instruments to muffle the voices of the audience. There were no solos highlighting a few gifted singers, but an emphasis on every individual praising God. It was the first place I felt like I could sing loud (and sometimes off-key) without being noticed—because everyone was singing. You couldn't help *"speaking to one another with psalms, hymns, and songs from the Spirit."* You just had to *"sing and make music from your heart to the Lord"* (Ephesians 5:19).

The buzz didn't end when the final amen was said; it just got louder. The same actions that happened before the service began again. When the service was over, no one left. I was used to attending churches where most people made a beeline for the door, hoping to beat the Baptists to an enticing lunch at the local steakhouse. But here, people stayed and fellowshipped. Finally, the janitors or the person responsible for locking the building had to kick everyone out. The same scenario played itself out at the Sunday evening services we had then. The only difference in the evening service was that it was typically only the Christians attending and not visitors like at the morning service. I quickly found out that Sunday or Wednesday services were not optional. They were just part of being a committed follower of Christ.

How does that compare with what we see now? Our services are markedly different now. In many places, Elvis has left the building...in other words, you don't walk into our services and feel that same kind of buzz. They are nice, but for the most part, pedestrian. To a degree, I don't sense that family-reunion feel; I certainly see few Bibles (or electronic versions of it) open and being used to instruct, counsel and disciple one another.

The singing definitely has a different vibrancy. More of the energy emanates from the stage than from the audience. There is more reliance on amplification, part singers, musical instruments, solos and even recorded musical accompaniment of songs to drive the worship. I recently attended a service where the power was out and I was shocked at the lack of spiritual energy in the singing. The lack of teaching the basics of singing and the expectation of every member to participate has become painfully clear. Our worship and singing have drifted slightly toward performances as opposed to every member speaking to one another in psalms, hymns and spiritual songs.

There is clearly a loss of commitment when it comes to attendance at meetings of the body. You see it reflected in many ways. People make it to church shortly before services and they don't have to be kicked out of the building because of too much fellowship afterwards. Survey it with your own eyes and not your own experience. Also in more than a few churches, the length of the service has been reduced. Church leaders feel that people are busy and visitors certainly don't want to sit through a long service. That thinking is coupled with the fact that few churches have anything like Sunday school (which was a staple of the Crossroads church), nor do we have nearly as many meetings as we once did.

Midweek services are no longer planned for everyone every week, and if we have Bible talks at all, they are held sporadically. In practice, some church functions have become optional for people (midweek services, devotionals, Bible talks and special teaching days being among them). We've lost the power that comes when everyone is unified committed to advancing the cause of Christ. Another example of this problem is illustrated when I attended a HOPE*worldwide* walk to raise money for the poor (something I've done with my children for the last five years). It was sponsored by a church with 600 members. The walk had an attendance of only 110 members; it was very disheartening. All this reflects a diminished commitment to the body of Christ, which is a foundational pillar from which ministry effectiveness comes. We are teaching less than ever before and missing out on the power that comes from being in the Word and building family and all the one-another opportunities that are produced by it.

Discipleship Then and Now

After our decision to die to ourselves and make Jesus Lord (Luke 9:23), discipleship (having a discipling partner or group) was the relationship tool that helps us put that decision into practice. It's how Jesus trained his twelve apostles and it is how Paul trained Timothy and others. In the early part of the book of Acts when the apostles were arrested, it was clear that they were not recent graduates of the School of Tyrannus or any school of theology. They were unschooled, ordinary men. What stood out and astonished Jewish leaders was the fact that these men had been with Jesus. Discipleship helps us to walk as Jesus did.

Both in Gainesville and later in Boston, I was set up with a discipleship partner within the first few weeks after arriving. In Boston, I vividly remember my ministry leader telling me, "You might be able to get into heaven without discipleship, but you can't get into this church without it!" Indeed, there was a deep and sincere commitment to discipleship. Whether it was peer-to-peer, group, or older-to-younger discipleship (all of which I benefited from in Boston), it was the catalyst that moved my faith, dreams and intentions into practical action. It was the tool that addressed my sins and weaknesses, reshaped my character into

Christlikeness and gave me vision for what I could become. I didn't always like it, but I always appreciated it. Though occasionally painful, it produced fruit in my life that was worth the sometimes unsettling nature of accountability that comes with discipleship.

Discipleship is the most important tool we have to help us carry out the difficult aspects of our Christian walk. Evangelism is a great example of that. For most disciples, evangelism is the most challenging aspect of their faith. Without the constant call, encouragement and accountability to share our faith, it quickly fades into obscurity and only those who are deemed to have the so-called "gift" of evangelism do it. Over the last decade as we have abandoned discipleship and the priority of evangelism (making disciples) has suffered along with it. We now struggle to attain even a 1% growth. If you subtract the number of baptisms that occur within families when teens are baptized (and those are important), the number of outsiders we are reaching is dismal. We are not nearly keeping up with world population growth. On average, the world's population increases by 210,000 every day (over 75 million a year), and our movement baptized barely over 7000 lost souls in all of 2015. Our evangelistic outreach and growth as a movement is dependent on discipleship. Without it, we will not reach our communities or the world.

The most disturbing aspect of our optional approach to discipleship is that we have created a double standard of membership in the Lord's church. You can be a totally committed and fired-up disciple of the Lord—and you will be encouraged, admired and accepted. You can also be half-hearted, uncommitted, disinterested or unevangelistic—and be accepted. Thus when new converts are made, Satan uses this dichotomy in a powerful way: he tries to convince young Christians that you can live either way and be accepted by God. When the church accepts what God doesn't, Satan rejoices. With the loss of a godly standard of biblical commitment, we become no different than the religions around us who have little or no biblical standards for membership. The entire body of Christ must be committed to the lordship of Jesus. Without discipleship, that simply will not happen.

Also because of the lack of discipleship in many ministries, about 20% of the congregation are doing 90% of the work. Those whose hearts are totally committed throw themselves into the work. But it becomes a spiritual drag when you feel like everyone is not on board with the mission. Eventually, these goodhearted disciples burn out. It also impacts full-time workers. Many staff members not only provide spiritual leadership, but carry a heavy load of office work, website design and administration, flyer design, finding places to meet and the list goes on. With this divided interest, the advancement of the kingdom through prayer and the ministry of the word is compromised (Acts 6:4).

The loss of discipleship has also caused a flourishing of support ministries. I'm not marginalizing the good work that is being done (I publish a number of books in this very area), but many of these needs were met when discipling relationships were functioning. We now have recovery groups, including sexual identity and or sexual purity recovery, chemical recovery, divorce recovery, grief processing groups, anger management groups, and a cottage industry of psychologists with more patients than time available to counsel them. This only reflects the society at large. We have all become victims in need of recovery as opposed to sinners who need forgiveness.

I have a close friend, a strong disciple, who now regularly sees a psychiatrist. I asked him why he was seeing him. He said, "Honestly, I now have a relationship with someone who listens to me and helps me. It's what I used to get in discipling times, but that's no longer available." I think he's right. There will always be the need for professional Christian mental health experts to meet more serious needs, and that's important. But genuine and close discipling relationships can solve and provide the help needed for the majority of us to deal with life's challenges.

It's obvious that I have serious concerns for the direction of our movement. I'm not alone; there are many who know we have problems but don't have the opportunity or forum to address them: and many have giving up doing so. Perhaps the present generation of leadership is past the point of rescue. Maybe a new generation of disciples will have to arise where we have compromised. But I do believe it can be turned around, and Gordon will suggest ways to do that in the following pages.

Chapter Fifteen

God Help Us With Solutions!

I don't want to end by just pointing out our problems (although they must be identified honestly). We do go to the doctor to be told the truth and find solutions, not to be patted on the head and told that we are just fine, if we are not. We must also want to hear the truth about our spiritual health, individually and collectively. However, I have to admit that I am like some of the prophets in the Old Testament were, in just condemning the sins and calling for repentance—without helping people know how to repent. I once was riding in a car with a dear ministry couple when the wife started preaching (fairly gently) to both me and her husband. She said that we preachers spoke about the need to have faith in order to please God, without helping the people know how to develop it. That was true and that is my tendency. We need help from others besides me, that's for sure. I am good with diagnoses (I think), but not so good in helping with effective cures. With that in mind, here are a few of my ideas about what can help with, but perhaps not totally solve, our problems.

The Holy Spirit and the War Room
In by book, *The Apostle Paul: Master Imitator of Christ*, I mention some teaching of Ed Anton. He is speaking more and more about how we have to learn to work in the power of the Holy Spirit. One of the striking points he made in Dallas recently was by means of what is said in Ephesians 5:18: *"Do not get drunk on wine, which leads to debauchery. Instead, be filled with the Spirit."* His main point was that the passage is not just telling us to replace the sin of drunkenness with being spiritual. A comparison is being made, namely that both drunkenness and being filled with the Spirit have a key element in common: both make you lose your inhibitions. If we are going to make the impact on this

world that God intends, we are going to have to be filled with the Spirit, lose our fears and inhibitions, and get on with sharing our faith and convictions with the lost and with each other.

How do we accomplish that? Although the answer involves several things, war-room-type prayer is at the head of the list. If you have not seen that movie, *War Room*, please see it. We must become intense prayer warriors. Further, we must restore true discipling, which is designed to help us become more and more like Christ. To be like him, we have to develop his character and heart, which leads to imitating his actions—and he clearly came into our world to seek and save those who were lost. If we are not doing that, we are not imitating Christ, but to do that zealously as he did, we have to raise our convictions and lose our inhibitions—and that must lead us to the war room of learning to pray like most of us have never learned to pray!

Build the Church into a Team

Recently I had a coffee time with our lead evangelist, Todd Asaad, and during our conversation I shared my convictions that we leaders had to get more input from our average members. They need to be able to express what they are seeing and thinking, and we need to be listening and learning from them. I mentioned that the Seattle church has a sister, Kelly Flores, with this very expertise, serving as a dean of a college that grants doctorates in the field of applied leadership. She developed a survey that the leaders I know in Seattle have raved about. She also happens to be my "adopted" daughter (read the two articles about our relationship on my website, www.gordonferguson.org). By that same evening, Todd had contacted both an evangelist in Seattle and Kelly. As a result, Todd had Kelly come to Dallas for several days and meet with the key leaders, after which she and they developed a survey that our church just took. She was brought back just this week to meet with the staff and explain more in detail what the survey taught us and where we should go from here in implementing changes.

Too many of our members think that we believe that we already know it all and don't care what they have to say. In many cases, they are spot-on accurate in this opinion. I am thankful to be a part of a congregation that is not in this category. We learned from the Seattle church; I pray that many churches learn from them and from Dallas. We must have ways to garner more input from our members, which helps them feel more a real part of the team and helps us learn from the team. The whole process helps us identify what people's gifts are and helps them put those gifts into practice in meaningful ways.

Since I mentioned Todd, I want to commend him for building team among the church staff and for setting an example in personal evangelism and helping the rest of the staff do the same. Our ministry staff is diverse in race and age, and almost to a person they are real characters. Todd knows how to work with different types of people well, and in his focus on our personal evangelism, he makes it about people and God, not numbers. His wife, Patty, has lupus and the limitations that go with it. Her attitude is that while she can't do some things that other women in her role might be able to do, she can reach out to her neighbors, and the Asaads have the most effective neighborhood evangelism outreach I have seen in decades. Building team means that you are a part of the team, doing precisely what you are calling others to do.

Structure and Accountability Are Your Friends

When I first starting associating with this movement, we were a fast-growing movement. My mainline Church of Christ friends would ask me how it was being done, as they were both mystified and envious. My initial impression, which was the answer I gave them, was that the members had a constant focus on evangelism and an accountability in place to keep it functioning. Perhaps these two words strike fear into the hearts of some disciples but, strangely, only when applied in a spiritual setting. We all believe in both when it comes to how we want our marriages, families and businesses to function. Consistently, functionality is based on these two things. Most of what we need to restore in our congregations cannot happen without both. The second law of thermodynamics states that everything in the world naturally goes from order to disorder. Just look at your desk or your lawn if you doubt. Organization is the antidote to such growing disorder.

However, it can become either legalism or highly fulfilling. The former causes the aforementioned negative reactions and the latter produces a warm feeling of accomplishment.

As I mentioned a couple of chapters back, I have written three books, with a total page count of about 600 pages, in less than four months. What did it take? Structure and accountability. I have been organized and worked hard, and Toney Mulhollan of IPI has provided the accountability by way of deadlines. So, what do you suppose I am feeling as I write this last chapter? Anger, frustration and negativity, or fulfillment and accomplishment? Our churches need structure and accountability (done correctly, not in the old or sinful ways). More important, they deserve it. It's past time for our leaders to get on board with this, don't you think? But by all means, get input from nonstaff members in order to do it well and to gain their buy-in. With Nike's trademark in mind—*Just Do It!*

Understand New Testament Leadership and Use It

In the past several years I have probably written and spoken more about leadership than any other subject, mostly at the request of other leaders. *Dynamic Leadership* is a complete book on it, and my recent book, *The Apostle Paul: Master Imitator of Christ*, has the longest of five parts on the subject as it examines Paul's approach to leadership. Although I think we still have much to learn about the topic (since many of our leaders mistakenly think they understand the subject well), one aspect of it did dawn on me fairly recently. I will include a quote from my Paul book here to help us learn together. Our churches will not get unstuck unless we understand the principles within as well as put them into practice. It is a long quote, but it will be worth the space and time needed to read it.

> One of our hindrances involving leadership is how we tend to view leadership. Of course, all of us are aware that we have small-group leaders or program leaders of many types, but we still think of the "real" leaders as being those on staff, with the possible addition of elders who aren't. But when you put yourself back into the first-century church setting, you quickly

realize that very few leaders would be like our ministry staff leaders today—paid by the church. We know that Paul received support financially from time to time, but he also worked at tent making to support himself. He argued that he had a right to be supported, as we saw in 1 Corinthians 9, and he also argued for elders (especially those who preached and taught) to be supported financially in 1 Timothy 5:17–18. However, one reason that they didn't have a clergy/laity feel to leadership was because of a lack of paid staff. I am not a member of a paid staff now, even on a part-time basis, but I was for decades. In our modern setting, I am totally supportive of our practice and appreciative of having been a part of it for years. However, one of the main drawbacks to the way we do it is the way we view it, with church-supported leaders being seen as the main leaders with any authority. That is, put quite simply, quite wrong.

Look at 1 Corinthians 16:15–16. The church was strongly encouraged to submit to the leadership of Stephanas and to such people and to everyone who joins in the work and labors at it. These were leaders in the church, but not staff leaders as we would think of it. That system was not yet developed. The word in Greek translated "submit" is a strong one (*hupotassō*), used also in James 4:7: **"Submit yourselves,** *then, to God. Resist the devil, and he will flee from you"* (emphasis added). This passage in 1 Corinthians 16 shows the natural ordering of leadership relationships in a developing church, and this same ordering is a continual necessity in any organization—including the church. Submission to leaders cannot mean just to those on the ministry staff!

Hebrews 13 can provide some valuable help along these lines. In verse 17 we read: *"Obey your leaders and submit to their authority. They keep watch over you as men who must give an account. Obey them so that their work will be a joy, not a burden, for that would be of no advantage to you"* (NIV 1984). Who were those leaders? Not just *staff* or *elders*, according to verse 7 of the same chapter: *"Remember your leaders, who spoke the word of God to you. Consider the outcome of their way of life and imitate their faith."* Do not our small-group leaders speak the word of God to the groups they lead? Of course they do! My biggest concern is that our paid staff leaders cannot possibly do all that needs to be done in the leadership realm. I know that harsh, worldly leadership is not Golden Rule leadership (Matthew 20:20-28). However, I also know that a failure to lead strongly and spiritually is not imitating Christ's leadership. Have we swung the pendulum of leading strongly in a worldly manner to not leading strongly even in a spiritual manner? Nonstaff leaders, do you know where your sheep are and how they are really doing? Bottom line—are we functioning like a *family*?[6]

God Will Have to Work Mightily—Perhaps Against the Grain

Buckle up your seat belts for this one—tight! When I was in the mainline church, it eventually dawned on me that we would never get the job done of world evangelism. I made the statement fairly often that if we didn't get it done, God would raise up someone else who would. On my first trip to the Florida Evangelism Seminar in August 1981, Chuck Lucas had all of the couples and individuals stand up who were already leading campus ministries or who were in training to do so. When that large group of young people and young couples stood up, the idea hit me that I was probably looking at those whom God was raising up to do what I had been predicting. They were young, idealistic and had a gleam in their eye that said they were going to do what needed to be done, no matter whether anyone else joined them or not. These young people were, in effect, young prophets (in spirit), and they actually did what hadn't been done in my lifetime and what most older people were saying could never be done.

We are approaching the stage now where the mainline churches were when I was a young minister. I've already described their decline and have mentioned what a seventy-year-old (Jim Woodruff) said a decade ago about them being in the last days of a dying movement. Others didn't like hearing what he said and wanted to find ways to look at their movement more positively. I think we are starting to follow the same pattern. I'm not suggesting that we are already a dying movement. However, looking at the statistics we examined in the previous chapter doesn't leave us with much wiggle room regarding the direction we are heading. In my opinion, we are going to have to face those facts before we can "faith" them and figure out ways to change them (move God to change them). Sometime last year, I received an email from a student in one of our campus ministries. I think he was leading a Bible talk at the time but wasn't on staff as an intern, yet he was very interested in the future of our movement. I was deeply moved by his letter and answered him as honestly as I could. I am now going to begin concluding this chapter by sharing his note to me and mine back to him. If you are a young person reading this interchange, this message is especially for you.

Dear Gordon,

I just finished reading *In Search of a City* and it got me thinking a lot. I love the history of our church. It really fascinates me. I wanted to ask you what you thought of a more centralized structure of leadership in the church. I never thought that one man calling the shots would be a very great system of church leadership. However, from my perspective I have felt like the structure of having a group of individuals leading the movement in a certain direction through team leadership could be, although at points difficult, very effective. I've been having conversations with leaders to try and understand various perspectives on what happened and where our church is going. The latter is what I care about most. My question is what do you feel our church is doing or needs to do to become a unified movement bent on evangelizing the world? Are there talks to unify the movement and have a common vision?

From my perspective, each church has a region and looks to their region leaders to see where the region leaders are leading the church (regionally). But outside of that there does not seem to be (at least from my perspective) a group of leaders that the movement can look to for seeing where the movement is heading. I don't know; I have just become very passionate about our movement having the feeling of being a "movement" once again. Although not THE modern-day movement of God, I would love for us to feel like we are A major modern-day movement of God. I would love to see well-respected leaders in our movement join forces to form some sort of structure to move things forward globally. What do you think will happen or can happen? Where do you think we are heading?

Dear Young Brother,

Well, you raised an extremely important and, to me, a very sensitive point in your note. I've been doing a lot of thinking about the same things lately, praying about them and worrying about them—all rolled up into one. What we had in the old days was an amazing unity of purpose to evangelize the world, driven in large part by the vision that traced back to Chuck Lucas in the Crossroads days and passed on to young, idealistic, talented people under him. As the focus moved to another man, this time in Boston, the vision was still there but the building methodology was biblically faulty and led us exactly where 1 Corinthians 3:10–15 said it would. In time, we rightly rejected an iron-grip type of leadership from one man, but somehow we lost the idea of a more centralized leadership that could keep us moving in a determined way.

One of the biggest issues (which some would cringe at hearing) is that we no longer had a visionary prophet to inspire us in ways that can really provide the impetus needed. Along with that vacuum came a focus on righting wrongs and in so doing, we became too afraid of allowing potential prophets to have that voice—out of fear that we would slip back into the old way. But the bad of the old way wasn't organization; it was method. In my earliest days in the movement (when in San Diego) I made the statement that if you took the two extremes of leadership possibilities (really hands-off and really strong, hands-on), the right kind of leadership is much closer to the really-strong end of the spectrum. Whether we are talking sports or business or any other organization, strong leadership is a must if we are to accomplish great things. Jesus was scary strong, but his strength as a leader was matched by his servant heart so that no one with that good and honest heart doubted his motives. He lit their flame and they followed to the death.

I don't think it can be done without prophet-type persons driving the vision and enlisting others who have similar gifts of vision and fearlessness in leading. The early apostles had these gifts, based on what was done in their generation. I'm sure not everyone (probably not even a majority) would agree with my assessment. But I recently made a call to a younger leader who has that wild side about him and what seems to me a prophet's spirit. I don't know him well, but my main message to him was not to let us older guys slow him down or stop him from being radical. To get back what you and I want to see, it is going to take the younger generation starting over in many ways—taking our good stuff, but also recreating a radical call to discipleship and world evangelism (including those next door to us and in the classroom and workplace with us). We went too long without stirring that spirit back up and now it is going to take a new generation to get it done. The older generation had their day and were used by God in great ways, but we are no longer there. We are happy with five percent growth per year because we are comparing ourselves with ourselves instead of comparing ourselves with Jesus and the early church.

I have criticized the mainline membership because they see baptism as fire insurance, much like the evangelical world sees "getting saved." They want to live nice, comfortable little lives and still go to heaven when they die. Now many (most?) of our members are of the same mindset, which results in a rejection of radical Christianity (shown by actions), the type of religion that our Founder clearly lived and died for. What should we do about it? You tell me. I could use the encouragement, honestly, because I often think of the words of the old song, "MacArthur Park": "I don't think that I can take it, 'cause it took so long to bake it, and I'll never have that recipe again—oh, no."[7] I used to think of our country when I heard that song, thinking back to a very moving presentation at Six Flags Over Texas when I was still a fairly young man. I thought to myself then, "My children and their children will never know the America that I was raised in." Now while I still have that feeling about our country, I also have it about our movement. But I desperately want to be wrong.

Please make me wrong, you and your generation. Appreciate and learn what you can from our generation, but do not let what we did form a ceiling for your generation. Make us and what we have done the foundation and build something we only dreamed about. God has both the desire and the power to make it happen, so all he needs are the right people. He's had them before in different generations, and he knows what they look and act like. He's looking for them now.

> *"Were not the Cushites and Libyans a mighty army with great numbers of chariots and horsemen? Yet when you relied on the LORD, he delivered them into your hand. For the eyes of the LORD range throughout the earth to strengthen those whose hearts are fully committed to him"* (2 Chronicles 16:8–9).

Are we doing it now? No. Can it be done? Yes. Will we do it once again? The answer to that one is within your generation, young man. That's what I think. Am I right? OGK (only God knows), but he will let it become known in time. Be a prophet yourself and enlist lots and lots of others to be the same. When in the mainline, I preached often that if we didn't get it done, God would raise up someone who would. He did—and he will again. Be a part of it.

Love,
Gordon

How does this email exchange strike you? Hopefully, if you are young, it helps light your fires. If you are older, I hope you have the wisdom and humility to admit that our generation has dropped the ball in world evangelism and must pass the baton to the younger generation and hold up their hands. In the case that you take offense at what I said, I don't mind that, if it drives you to really consider the point I am making. This is the third movement of which I have been a part, so I've been to this rodeo before. I recognize characteristics and trends pretty well by now, and I believe that we have a problem—a growing one. If you disagree, prove me wrong. Nothing would make me happier than to be wrong about what I think I am seeing. I love you whether you agree with me or not. My opinions aren't going to stop me from being the best disciple of Christ that I can, or stop me from helping others be the best they can be, or stop me from making new disciples. Nothing about my convictions or practices is going to change. This isn't about me and it isn't about you and it isn't about our movement, really. It is about God. Let's love God and make him happy, and if we can seriously focus on that, he can help us out of the concerning situation in which we find ourselves. He is the relentless pursuer of souls. Let's allow him to be that with us in every area of our lives. That cannot possibly be wrong, whether my assessments are right or wrong.

An Other-Worldly Focus

In different ways, I have said repeatedly that we must have an other-worldly focus, not only to make a serious impact in reaching the lost world, but to please God and go to heaven. We desperately need to see the essentiality of imitating Christ, in his character, his heart and his actions. We express this concept so often that it loses its impact on us. 1 John 2:6 could hardly be clearer: *"Whoever claims to live in him must walk as Jesus did."* He doesn't say should walk as Christ; he says must. It is a salvation issue, and passages could be multiplied that make the same point—very pointedly. I'm not suggesting a performance based salvation here, for none of us imitates Jesus perfectly. But it is a matter of having a heart set on imitating Jesus and a life that shows clearly that doing such is our top priority. As one old preacher put it, the concept of total commitment is the perfect commitment of an imperfect life.

To start this list of solutions in the beginning of this chapter, I spoke of being filled with the Holy Spirit in a way that few of us grasp even in concept, much less in practice. It too lies in that other-worldly realm. Bottom line, we are far too much a part of this world and too focused on it. One of C.S. Lewis' many famous quotes hit this nail on the head: "If you read history you will find that the Christians who did most for the present world were precisely those who thought most of the next. It is since Christians have largely ceased to think of the other world that they have become so ineffective in this." According to Ephesians 2:6, disciples have already entered the heavenly realms with Christ. Yet, for most who call themselves Christians, you would never know it because we are still caught up in this present world. Few grasp the spiritual realm as a present reality in the way that passage after passage says that we should, both seeing it and living in it. We are in the world but are not to be of it. Honestly, we are in it and also of it in ways that we do not fully comprehend.

I am going to close this chapter and this book with scripture quotations that I beg you to not just skim over, but to read slowly, carefully and repeatedly. Then journal about what you read, looking carefully at your own life and comparing it to what these verses say. 2 Corinthians 13:5 tells us that it is time for some serious personal examination: *"Examine yourselves to see whether you are in the faith; test yourselves. Do you not realize that Christ Jesus is in you—unless, of course, you fail the test?"* If we do this, it will of necessity drive us to our knees before an Almighty God who must be taken seriously, more seriously than most perceive. Please do it. Rest assured that I'm doing it with you, and have started well before this book came off the press.

When I started writing this book, I expected it to be a fun process, doing some reminiscing and rejoicing about my three lives. What happened is that I end it being more convicted that I could have imagined. Life is serious, death is real and heaven is eternal. Let's get ready for it — together. I love you.

1 John 2:15-17

[15]Do not love the world or anything in the world. If anyone loves the world, love for the Father is not in them. [16]For everything in the world—the lust of the flesh, the lust of the eyes, and the pride of

life—comes not from the Father but from the world. ^{17}The world and its desires pass away, but whoever does the will of God lives forever.

2 Timothy 2:3-4
^{3}Join with me in suffering, like a good soldier of Christ Jesus. ^{4}No one serving as a soldier gets entangled in civilian affairs, but rather tries to please his commanding officer.

James 4:2-4
^{2}You desire but do not have, so you kill. You covet but you cannot get what you want, so you quarrel and fight. You do not have because you do not ask God. ^{3}When you ask, you do not receive, because you ask with wrong motives, that you may spend what you get on your pleasures. ^{4}You adulterous people, don't you know that friendship with the world means enmity against God? Therefore, anyone who chooses to be a friend of the world becomes an enemy of God.

Colossians 3:1-3
^{1}Since, then, you have been raised with Christ, set your hearts on things above, where Christ is, seated at the right hand of God. ^{2}Set your minds on things above, not on earthly things. ^{3}For you died, and your life is now hidden with Christ in God.

John 17:14-16
^{14}I have given them your word and the world has hated them, for they are not of the world any more than I am of the world. ^{15}My prayer is not that you take them out of the world but that you protect them from the evil one. ^{16}They are not of the world, even as I am not of it.

2 Corinthians 4:16-18
^{16}Therefore we do not lose heart. Though outwardly we are wasting away, yet inwardly we are being renewed day by day. ^{17}For our light and momentary troubles are achieving for us an eternal glory that far outweighs them all. ^{18}So we fix our eyes not on what is seen, but on what is unseen, since what is seen is temporary, but what is unseen is eternal.

Philippians 3:20
²⁰*But our citizenship is in heaven. And we eagerly await a Savior from there, the Lord Jesus Christ...*

1 Peter 1:17
¹⁷*Since you call on a Father who judges each person's work impartially, live out your time as foreigners here in reverent fear.*

2 Peter 3:10-13
¹⁰*But the day of the Lord will come like a thief. The heavens will disappear with a roar; the elements will be destroyed by fire, and the earth and everything done in it will be laid bare.* ¹¹*Since everything will be destroyed in this way, what kind of people ought you to be? You ought to live holy and godly lives* ¹²*as you look forward to the day of God and speed its coming. That day will bring about the destruction of the heavens by fire, and the elements will melt in the heat.* ¹³*But in keeping with his promise we are looking forward to a new heaven and a new earth, where righteousness dwells.*

Hebrews 11:13-16
¹³*All these people were still living by faith when they died. They did not receive the things promised; they only saw them and welcomed them from a distance, admitting that they were foreigners and strangers on earth.* ¹⁴*People who say such things show that they are looking for a country of their own.* ¹⁵*If they had been thinking of the country they had left, they would have had opportunity to return.* ¹⁶*Instead, they were longing for a better country—a heavenly one. Therefore God is not ashamed to be called their God, for he has prepared a city for them.*

---

6. Gordon Ferguson, *The Apostle Paul: Master Imitator of Christ*, Illumination Publishers, Spring, Texas.

7. Jimmy Webb, "MacArthur Park" (Los Angeles, CA: Dunhill Records, 1968).

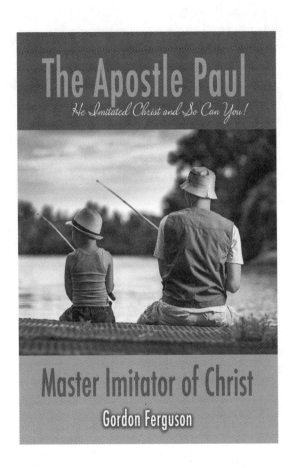

www.ipibooks.com

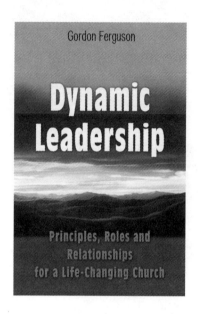
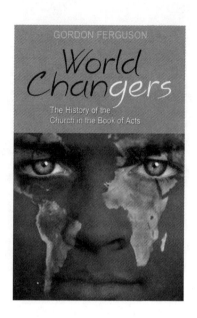

www.ipibooks.com

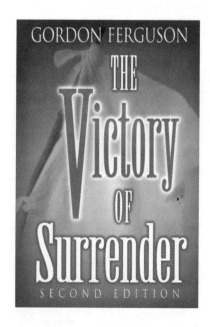
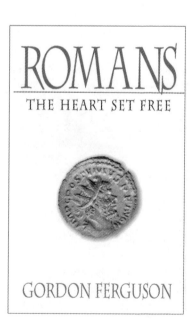

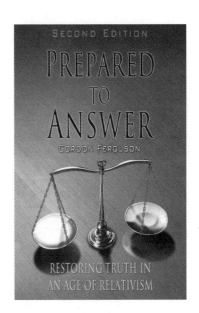

www.ipibooks.com

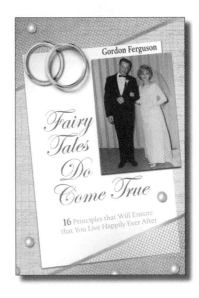

www.ipibooks.com